# BOATS FOR SAILING

Boats for Sailing

by Ian Proctor MSIA

A Design Centre Publication

Macdonald & Co (Publishers) Ltd in association with the Council of Industrial Design 1968

# Contents

A family racing boat. One of the 15′ 7″
Kestrel Class, designed by Ian Proctor
Photographer: John Etches

# Introduction

In these days, almost all sailing boats are meant for pleasure. They are not used commercially for fishing or transportation from A to B, but just for recreation.

This seemingly single role is not as simple as may at first appear, because boats are enjoyed in dozens of different ways. To some, boats are simply the instruments on which they can use their sailing skills competitively—the racing fanatics for whom everything must take second place to speed and the ability to win. To others, they are possessions so cherished that they rarely go afloat except in ideal conditions. Some enjoy building them more than sailing them; others buy a new boat every year rather than bother with any maintenance work. Some want to take their families afloat with them; others find they like them better if they are left ashore till after racing is over.

The right boat for one enthusiast may be quite wrong for another. But, whatever type of enjoyment she is supposed to give, correct design for the intended function is of prime importance. The choice is very varied and claims for each may add to the difficulties of the bewildered purchaser. The aim of this book is to assist towards deciding what to look for in a boat and to indicate what will help a boat give you the kind of fun you want from it, in safety.

# 1 Function

It is a strange fact that nearly all sailing boats stir the competitive spirit. Types designed originally with comparatively little thought of speed are inevitably raced, but seldom can provide the same satisfaction through responsiveness or handiness as a boat specifically intended for racing. There are many good compromises with a high degree of versatility, but it is wise to decide what the prime function of your boat will be and to choose one with the emphasis firmly on character-istics suitable for that use.

This may seem obvious, yet often boats of comparatively stolid and uninteresting performance are used primarily for racing and equally frequently boats with lively and skittish characteristics are used for family sailing, though they do little to inspire confidence in children or novices.

In general, sailing boats can be divided into five categories—with some hybrids between them.

## a Out-and-out racing

Sailing boats designed specifically for racing are usually the result of a great deal of specialised thought, not exclusively directed at speed, but also concerned with ease of handling, seaworthiness and safety. In fact, all recognised racing classes have stringent buoyancy and safety rules, and often rules ensuring constructional strength, sometimes overlooked in non-racing types which are not necessarily backed by any class organisation or national authority.

The factors producing the speed sought in racing boats conflict with the characteristics desirable in a boat for more leisurely sailing. The main factors for speed are:

1 Generous driving power derived from the wind by relatively large sail area.

2 Light-weight hull and spars reducing the displacement of the hull and increasing planing ability.

3 Hull shape of low wave-making resistance at moderate speeds, primarily attained through limiting waterline beam and by slim and easy underwater lines.

4 Low frictional resistance attained by reducing wetted surface area (area of hull in contact with water).

5 Hull shape producing dynamic lift and low drag at high speeds to promote planing.

Each of these factors (except 5) tends to make the boat less stable in fresh winds.

Racing boat hulls normally, but not invariably, show a marked decrease in efficiency if loaded in excess of their designed displacement—and this designed load is probably none too generous and not greater than the hull is normally likely to carry when racing.

Stability and power to carry the big sail area of racing boats is provided principally by the counterbalancing movement of the weight of the helmsman and crew. Whether the boat remains upright depends largely upon their skill, agility and endurance. Some racing boats have various aids to increase the effect of the weight of helmsman and crew as live ballast; these are dealt with later.

A racing boat is likely to be wetter to sail in than other types, partly because of her speed, but also because she has lower freeboard (less depth of hull above water level) and because, in the design of the hull, speed will not have been sacrificed to considerations of keeping the spray down.

Speed itself can produce handling difficulties, particularly in very restricted and crowded waters. Rough water sailing is also more difficult in most fast boats when reaching or running, as the effects of being thrown off course or into a different state of trim by waves when travelling at high speed calls for very quick reactions on helm and sheets and rapid shifting of crew weight to avoid capsize. Fast boats often have small rudders (to reduce wetted surface to a minimum) and less directionally stable hull forms. A good racing boat will, of course, be quite controllable in skilled hands under most conditions, but sailing in fresh winds and rough water demands alertness and there is little opportunity for relaxing. This is what the racing crew likes, but may not suit those who want more carefree progress.

Visibility in a racing boat can also be much reduced by very low footed jibs and, though plastic windows may be provided in these, they only give a limited view, so that constant vigilance is necessary to avoid collisions.

## b Family racing

This category includes some boats of quite good racing performance. To get the very best performance from them they also make demands on the energy and endurance of the crew but, in contrast to the out-and-out racing types, can be sailed quite satisfactorily without much effort. They carry less sail area and are rather beamier and usually more heavily built. Frequently more attention is paid to comfort when sailing, but this is by no means always the case, as crew comfort is also of prime importance in a top performing racing boat, to increase physical endurance and efficiency.

There may be lockers and dry stowage for gear, which would be lacking in an out-and-out racing boat. It may also be possible to row or use an outboard engine, which would be taboo in the other type. Generally speaking, however, not many concessions will be made to anything other than space and stability.

## c Cruising and general purpose

This type is more stable than either of the other two. The hull is beamier and relatively heavy, and the sail plan is low in height and area. There should be more space in the boat, with room for stowing gear and usually for carrying an outboard engine or even camping and sleeping gear.

Such a boat is comparatively slow, but does not demand much activity on the part of the crew in moderate weather. The extra weight may make it difficult to handle the boat out of the water and launching may be more of a problem unless a good slipway is available.

## d Single handers

1 Sailing surfboards or developments of them

Sailing surfboards, of which the several variants of the Minisail are examples in this country and the Sailfish is a very popular example in the USA, are relatively cheap, and though wet, probably give more fun and excitement per pound in cost than any other type. They are usually almost completely decked and unswampable, although some have small cockpits. Those without cockpits (such as the Minisail Monaco Mark I) usually have a dished deck, from which the spray drains into the daggerboard case or simply over the stern. Some find

6

# Out-and-out racing type

a  High aspect ratio mainsail of large area
b  Large spinnaker, possibly bigger than mainsail
c  Large low-footed jib, set from high point
d  No coaming on foredeck, reduces wind resistance
e  Low freeboard, reduces wind resistance
f  Smaller rudder, for low wetted surface area
g  Deep centreboard gives good lateral resistance
h  Crew has to lie far out, parallel to water
i  Fine bow sections, for low resistance in waves, allows bow wave
   to run up hull and blow aboard
j  Side pressure on deep centreboard causes strong heeling force

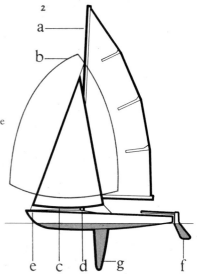

# Family racing type

a  Moderate aspect ratio of mainsail of moderate area
b  Moderate size spinnaker
c  Moderate, short-footed jib, set from lower point
d  Coaming diverts spray off foredeck
e  Fairly high freeboard
f  Larger rudder for easier control
g  Shallow centreboard, operating in less deep water, requires
   greater area for equal lateral resistance
h  Crew sit on gunwale (can lie out if energetic)
i  Fuller, flared bow sections turn down bow wave
j  Side pressure on shallower centreboard causes less strong
   heeling forces

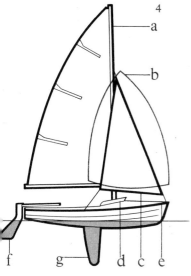

# Cruising type

a  Low aspect ratio mainsail of small area
b  No spinnaker
c  Small, short-footed jib
d  High coaming to keep spray out of cockpit
e  High freeboard
f  Deeper rudder necessary as wide stern tends to lift as boat heels,
   raising rudder out of water. Greater resistance
g  Greater lateral area required as fuller bows are pushed more
   easily to leeward by waves. May be heavy metal plate to aid
   stability
h  Crew can sit in boat (can lie out if energetic)
i  Full bow sections produce big bow wave, but high freeboard
   keeps it off deck
j  Side pressure at end of centreplate causing heeling force is
   counteracted by weight of centreplate causing righting force

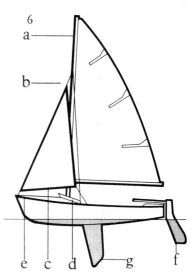

that this type of deck does not give a feeling of great security and prefer to have a small foot well, as in the Minisail Monaco Mark II. This also makes it easier to change position when tacking. The Minisail can carry a short sliding seat to help hold it upright in fresh winds. Most boats of this type are reasonably long for their weight and, though narrow, are relatively quite wide at the waterline, so that they are able to carry two people without ruining their performance. They are not usually very fast to windward, but some of them have an excellent performance reaching and running and, due to their low freeboard, give a very satisfying impression of speed.

Rigs vary, but most only carry a mainsail. Simplicity of rig is important and both the spars and boat can be easily carried on a car roof rack. In the British climate, a wet-suit is the most suitable garb to wear in these boats, but not essential of course.

2 Dinghies or canoes of light displacement, usually with simple and easily handled rigs

Single-handed dinghies generally vary from about 12 to 15 feet in length and their performance suffers if loaded with more than one person. The spars and rigging are designed to take the loads imposed by sailing single-handed and may be overstrained by sailing two-up. In the Finn and OK dinghies, for instance, the mast is completely unstayed with no supporting rigging and is unlikely to survive the loads imposed if two people sail the boat in fresh winds.

The very sophisticated Ten Square Metre Canoe is a highly specialised craft calling for great skill, and is rather limited in its appeal, partially due to high cost. Its performance is fantastic. These boats are among the fastest single hulled craft afloat. They are extremely narrow and unstable but very thrilling.

## e Catamarans

These are outside the scope of this book and will not be dealt with in detail here. Because, in effect, they provide a sailing platform with great beam, and hence stability, while at the same time each individual hull has very little beam and wave-making resistance, the speed of catamarans in moderate and fresh winds is greater than that of mono-hulls. The two hulls together have greater wetted-surface area than most monohulls of similar length, so that frictional resistance is greater and speed in light airs is less. The fact that the two hulls are separate causes greater resistance when they are turned sharply, and they are not very good when short tacking in confined spaces.

# 2 Construction
## a Materials and methods

The two principal materials used in boat construction are timber and glass reinforced plastic (GRP). The latter is becoming increasingly

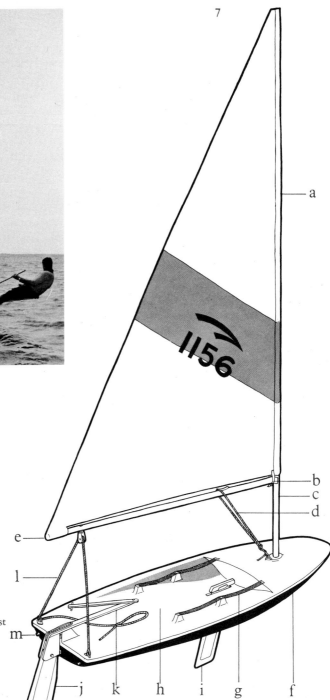

Unit, a single-hander
designed by David Thomas,
showing the use of sliding
seat and long tiller extension

a Sail sleeved on to mast
b Tape ties sail to boom
c Jointed aluminium tubular mast
d Kicking strap holds boom to mast
e Sail sleeved on to boom
f GRP or timber hull, with foam
  buoyancy
g Toe-straps
h Self-draining deck
i Daggerboard
j Lifting rudder
k Tiller with extension
l Main sheet
m Drain plugs

Minisail, a high performance sailing
surfboard, designed by Ian Proctor

popular for professionally built boats, and in the USA and some continental countries is used almost universally. When timber is used, it is almost invariably in laminated form for the main part of the structure. This may either be as plywood or as a built-up laminate formed to the shape of the boat by applying two or three layers of timber veneer over a mould, each layer of veneer running at a different angle and being bonded to adjacent veneers by waterproof synthetic resin glue. The veneers may be temporarily held in place by staples during the curing of the adhesive (the cold-mould process) or the skin of the hull, on its mould, may be put into a large cylinder which is sealed and steam-heated under pressure to form the laminate (the hot-mould process).

Hot-moulding timber is only suitable where long production runs off one hull shape are involved, as the equipment is costly and beyond the resources of the normal boat builder. Cold-moulding is suitable for short runs and individual boats and is used in particular for some very high quality racing boats. The method is expensive, but results in very strong and light-weight structures.

The commonest form of timber construction is from plywood panels. There may be two panels per side—one on the bottom and one on the topsides—and this is known as 'hard chine'. Or there may be three panels per side, known as 'double chine'. Or there may be four or more panels and the edges of each panel may overlap, as in the modern clinker-built Ospreys and Merlin-Rockets. The advantage of plywood, as opposed to solid timber for planking, is that wide panels can be used without fear of splits. If the correct type of plywood is used (BS1088) of good quality timber with outer laminations of equal thickness to the core, this material is very tough and long-lived.

GRP mouldings for hulls, decks and other components are usually produced by forming a laminate in an outside mould (contact moulding). The mould itself is usually a GRP laminate, which is formed over a very carefully made and highly polished 'plug' or pattern to the exact shape of the final moulding required.

The principal ingredients of a GRP laminate for boatbuilding are polyester resin and glassfibre of minute thickness (one-tenth the thickness of a hair) formed into strands. The resin, which has little tensile or impact strength on its own, is primarily to bond the glassfibre reinforcements into a homogeneous mass. Glassfibre is used as the reinforcement because it has good mechanical strength, is very stable under extremes of temperature and humidity, has low water absorption and does not deteriorate or perish.

The glassfibre may be in several forms.

1  Chopped strand mat. Composed of strands between 1 inch and 2 inches long held together in random form with a binder. Of relatively low cost, it is the most important form of reinforcement.
2  Rovings. Untwisted strands of glassfibre.

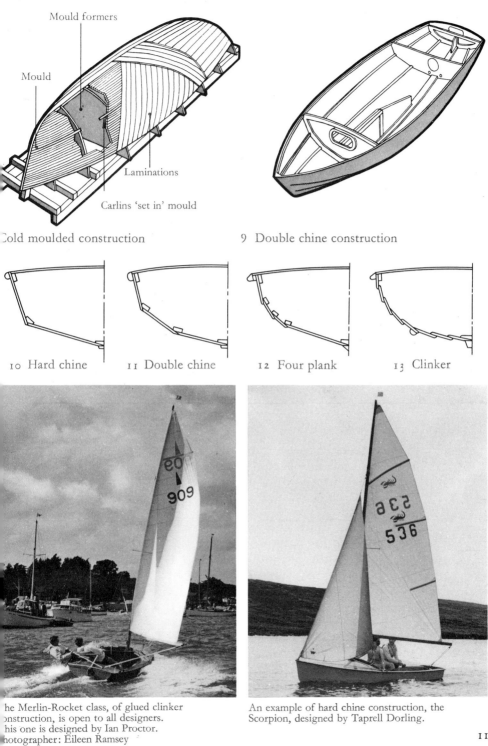

Mould formers

Mould

Laminations

Carlins 'set in' mould

Cold moulded construction

9 Double chine construction

10 Hard chine      11 Double chine      12 Four plank      13 Clinker

The Merlin-Rocket class, of glued clinker construction, is open to all designers. This one is designed by Ian Proctor.
Photographer: Eileen Ramsey

An example of hard chine construction, the Scorpion, designed by Taprell Dorling.

3   Woven rovings. Woven cloth of untwisted strands of glassfibre.
    More expensive than mat.
4   Cloths. Expensive and not much used.
5   Tapes. Woven glass cloth in narrow widths.
6   Surfacing tissues. Very fine cloths.

Chopped strand mats are used principally in all boat-building laminates, but impact and tensile strength can be greatly increased by using woven rovings, particularly on the inner side of the laminate. The mats should be applied in several layers, with the joints between the mats staggered so that they are reinforced by subsequent layers.

In the hand lay-up process a gel coat of pigmented resin is first brushed or sprayed onto the mould to give a good exterior finish. Sometimes this is followed by a veil tissue to help prevent the pattern of the mat showing through. Several layers of mat or woven rovings follow, being impregnated with pigmented resin by brushes and rollers used by hand. This method gives a rough texture internally and a surface tissue may be applied to smooth it off.

A new method, using matched moulds, has recently been introduced for producing GRP boats. In this, the cold-press method, strong moulds are made to give the external and internal shape and when they are brought together the gap between them gives the thickness of the moulding to be produced. The moulding is formed by draping the reinforcement over the internal mould, adding the resin and closing the external mould over it under considerable hydraulic pressure. Special design of the moulds causes excess resin to be squeezed out just before the moulds close completely to form the 'pinch off'. Very strong mouldings can be formed in this way, but a gel coat is not usually applied, so that the surface finish is not as shiny as with hand lay up.

There is a limitation to size at present and the 7' 6" Jiffy dinghy is the only boat produced by this method up to date. Between two and three Jiffy hulls can be moulded in an hour and costs are much reduced.

The flexibility of a GRP laminate is similar to that of marine plywood of equal thickness, though its tensile strength is at least four times greater. Its weight per cubic foot is about $2\frac{1}{4}$ times as much, so that, in order to produce a boat of equal weight to a wooden one, the hull skin must usually be of about half the thickness in wood. From the strength point of view, this presents no problems, but it may be over-flexible. This can be overcome by stiffening with ribs or stringers formed from GRP over plastic foam, metal, wood or even cardboard formers (the strength of the ribs is in the GRP, not the former itself).

Sometimes stiffness is obtained by backing up the laminate with balsa wood squares or plastic foam, either in sheet form, or actually foamed *in situ*. In the latter case the hull may be of two skins, with the foam introduced between the skins as a frothing liquid, which later sets. There are technical difficulties to this method, the pressure exerted by the foam being liable to cause distortions and voids which provide no stiffening. Though closed cell foam is normally used, as opposed to intercellular foam, which is quite unsuitable, there is likelihood of permanent entrapment of a certain amount of water if there is any leakage through the GRP skin.

There is also one basic snag to foam-stiffened small boat hulls. Because double-skinning is obviously bound to involve extra weight and the foam material itself, though very light, also adds weight, there is a tendency to reduce the GRP skin thickness. What is often produced, therefore, is a very thin GRP skin, held rigidly against any blow, instead of a comparatively thick skin, able to flex or spring away from a blow. In larger boats, with thicker skins, this is no problem; in small boats it may create difficulties.

There are various ways of building up hulls from sheets of expanded or foamed plastics, which can be heated and formed to shape, then sheathed on both sides with GRP. This is likely to be more satisfactory than double skinning first and foaming *in situ*, but there is then the difficulty of producing smooth exposed surfaces. On substantially flat surfaces, the one GRP skin can be formed against a mould and the foamed material applied to it with a coating of resin while the GRP laminate is still wet—thus obtaining one smooth face to the structure.

A relatively new material from the plastics industry now successfully used in boatbuilding is Acrylonitrile-Butadiene-Styrene (ABS), a thermoplastic capable of being vacuum formed in comparatively inexpensive moulds from sheet. It is highly resistant to abrasion, but has to be stiffened, and hulls of this material are usually double-skinned, with a relatively thick core of polyurethane foam between. The polyurethane is foamed *in situ*, the skins being heated as the foam is injected between them, technically a very difficult operation to carry out with entire success and freedom from voids or concentrations of pressure causing distortions. The completed foamed structure is light-weight—a 7' dinghy weighs only about 60 lbs—and has sufficient buoyancy in the hull skin itself to enable the boat to be chopped in half and still float a passenger. ABS is susceptible to deterioration in ultra-violet light (sun-light) but this can be largely overcome by pigmentation.

High density polyethylene is another plastic material now used for boatbuilding. Polypropylene, a thermoplastic polymeric material, may also have useful applications for boat building.

Aluminium alloy has been used for sailing boat hulls for many years without gaining significant popularity, and its chances of doing so are less now that GRP production is better understood. Though extremely tough and resistant to serious damage, the thinness of the skin necessary to keep weight within reasonable bounds, makes the hulls susceptible to denting. It is hard to disguise the material and combat the common appellation of 'tin boat'.

# b Do-it-yourself

Most boats designed for amateur construction are basically built up from large plywood panels and are hard chine, double chine or four-plank construction. If you wish to build your own boat, therefore, you will be limited to one of these forms of construction. Even within these limitations, the ease with which various designs may be built differs considerably and different degrees of skill are required. Some may be built from scratch, but others only from prefabricated kits of parts (often because the design has been licensed to a boatbuilder). The detail and clarity of plans and building instructions varies and has a considerable effect on the ease with which the boats can be built.

A simple form of construction recently evolved by Jack Holt and Barry Bucknell for the 10′ 10″ Mirror dinghy is of shaped plywood panels temporarily laced together at the edges by copper wire, the joint then being bonded on the inside with glassfibre tape and synthetic resin. The shape of the edges of adjacent panels, when drawn together, causes the panels to bend into the curves of the hull and no jig or mould is required to give the hull its form. The protruding ends of the wires on the outside are then cut off and filed down smooth, and layers of glassfibre tape and resin are applied outside the joint. The structure is reinforced by bulkheads and buoyancy chambers all bonded in with synthetic resin and glassfibre tape to form a very light structure weighing only 98 lbs. Building from scratch is not permitted, but kits of prefabricated parts and building instructions are readily available.

Another extremely simple construction, in which the edge of one component panel gives curvature to its neighbouring panel, is the 12′ 5″ SigneT, one of my own designs. It can be built from scratch or prefabricated kits of parts, full size plans of every component and detailed building instructions being available. In this construction the panels are joined by gluing and screwing into a longitudinal member called a chine stringer. The chine stringers (and keel and bilge rubbers) are first fastened to the bottom panel of the hull (flat bottomed); the buoyancy tank faces are then fastened to these stringers, their lower edges forcing the bottom panel into a curve. Transverse bulkheads are added, and a small longitudinal bulkhead aft and simple framework forward completes the curvature of the bottom, which is reinforced by the lower edge of the centreboard casing. The hull is thus virtually shaped before the sides and decking are added, and all joints are extremely simple to make, as there are none with changing bevels (angles). An extremely robust hull results, but the weight is about 55 lbs more than that of the Mirror dinghy.

In other cases, the panels are glued to a light, previously formed framework of keel, hog, stem, transom, stringers and gunwales, these components being supported either temporarily during building by frames which are later removed, or by permanent frames or bulkheads

## Method of building Mirror dinghy

## Method of building SigneT dinghy

14

Wiring plank edges together

Covering seams with glass
tape and resin

Cutting off excess wire

15

a  Bottom plank and chines

b  Cockpit sides and bottom give
   shape to one another

c  Assembly prior to decking

Mirror                    Designer: Jack Holt
                          Photographer: Eileen Ramsay

SigneT        Designer: Ian Proctor
              Photographer: Eileen Ramsay

which remain as part of the structure. In some cases this may be a relatively difficult method, as the angle between the adjacent outer sides of the stringers may change along the length of the boat and care must be taken to get these angles right, because the watertightness of the hull depends on a good joint being made between the stringer and the panels. Very robust hulls can be made by this method, particularly when permanent bulkheads are used, as in the 12' 6" Graduate, 11' Gull or 16' Wayfarer.

Glued-clinker construction is sometimes tackled by amateurs, but this requires considerably more skill. A compromise between a clinker and chine construction is used in the case of the 17' 6" Osprey and has some of the advantages of both methods for amateur building, giving the effect of round bilge hull shape with even greater ease of construction than double-chine, because the closeness of the stringers makes their bevelling a simple and sure procedure.

Cold-moulding is also sometimes done by amateurs. It is not particularly difficult and possibly requires less skill than some of the less sophisticated forms of construction, but takes much time and patience.

Boats designed for amateur construction are frequently slightly heavier than those intended almost exclusively for professional building, because simplification of construction for relatively unskilled builders, and the use of more easily made joints, tends to involve more material.

## c Cost

The cost differential of various forms of construction alters according to whether the boat is professionally or amateur built. Some forms of construction suitable for amateurs are time-consuming when skilled professionals with efficient woodworking machinery are involved, and therefore more costly.

It is also important to remember that, in order to keep down costs, the professional builder must in particular reduce labour costs as much as possible and costs of materials are relatively less important—exactly the reverse is the case with an amateur builder, who does not count the cost of his time.

Professional builders can usually construct a bare hull very quickly and economically and it is the finishing and fitting out which consumes time. For this reason it is often very worthwhile to buy a partially assembled kit, or even one completely assembled and ready for painting, and fit it out and finish it off yourself.

Generally, GRP boats are slightly more expensive than their wooden counterparts. The labour costs in GRP construction are comparatively low, but material costs are higher. The cost of moulds and development work is much higher, but if these can be spread over a long production run, the cost per boat may be quite small. The comparative cost of GRP materials has tended to lessen over the past few years and this form of construction is far more competitive in price than hitherto. Newly developed moulding techniques and more design experience are also reducing costs and improving the product.

## d Maintenance

Though the first cost of a GRP boat may be slightly more than a timber one, the maintenance costs are very much lower. In fact, they may be almost negligible.

Wooden boats require a good deal of maintenance and have to be protected by boat covers to avoid rapid deterioration. The cost of an efficient boat cover may well be more than the price differential between a wooden and GRP boat.

GRP is particularly suitable for the structure of boats with enclosed buoyancy tanks, as it is rot-proof. Enclosed buoyancy tanks in wooden boats become damp·and, as repainting inside the tanks is often impractical, are a likely site for rot and water soakage. The fairly common composite construction, with GRP hull skin, but wooden deck, built-in bulkheads and buoyancy tanks is, therefore, not a sound combination of materials, particularly as GRP hull shells are liable to condensation on the internal surface, so that the tanks are almost always damp. The main reasons for the choice of this composite construction are that amateurs can complete professionally-produced fibreglass hull shells and there is often also a feeling that a wood-decked boat is more pleasing aesthetically. It is often claimed, sometimes justifiably, that total GRP construction produces a boat looking like a piece of bathroom equipment. Good design should, however, eliminate the taunt 'Where are you going to put the taps?'

Whatever form of construction is chosen, drainage from the hull when the boat is ashore should be good and no pockets of water should be formed. This, of course, is very important in a wooden boat, nooks and crannies being particularly bad for harbouring dirt and moisture and forming a site for the deterioration of paint or varnish and subsequent water absorption.

You should reckon on varnishing or painting a wooden boat at least once a year. Modern synthetic materials have reduced maintenance work slightly and produce a tougher protective surface, but once these surfaces have been damaged, and moisture can get at the timber beneath, deterioration is as rapid as ever and may even be faster.

Unquestionably fibreglass is far easier and more economical to maintain, particularly if the boat is left afloat on moorings. The only instance when fibreglass may call for greater maintenance costs than timber is when the boat has frequently to be hauled over a shingle beach or other rough surfaces from which it cannot be protected. This, of course, damages both a wooden or a fibreglass hull, but the wood is more easily refurbished.

# 3 Trailer or Car Top

One of the attractions of small boat sailing is the ease with which the boat can be taken to different sailing sites. You can race against new competition, meet new friends, explore new waters every week-end if you wish.

Boats are transported either on trailers or on roof-racks above the car. Trailers are very easily towed and are no real problem with any car with brakes in good order. Roof-racks are cheaper and do not affect the speed limit, which with trailers is 40 mph in Britain, but although boats even as big as Flying Dutchman (19 feet 10 inches) are sometimes car-topped on special frameworks, a reasonable limit for car-topping is a hull weight of 180 lbs and length of 13 feet 6 inches. (This of course varies with different types of car.) The choice of roof-rack or trailer can, therefore, to some extent, influence the choice of boat.

# 4 Launching

Boats of 14 feet and less can normally be man-handled into the water reasonably easily. Those over 14 feet will probably need a launching trolley—a slight added expense.

# 5 Class Function

Though nothing to do with the design of a racing boat, the class organisation has an important practical effect on her functional capability. In fact, it is true that some poorly designed boats are successful in classes because of efficient class organisation—and other good designs fail for lack of it.

A class organisation makes and enforces the rules governing the boat and controls the running of the class. The main objects of the rules concerning the boats are to ensure they can be raced on more or less even terms, that they are soundly built (so that replacement boats are not a frequent necessity and that no one gains an advantage from having very expensive, but perhaps fragile and short-lived, equipment) and that the safety standards of buoyancy apparatus are adequate.

In addition, an active class organisation arranges Class Championships and other race meetings, liaises with the yachting press on publicity, gives technical advice to builders and prospective owners and produces a class handbook giving names of owners and information on where the class is sailed. In some cases, Class Associations work in conjunction with the Royal Yachting Association or International Yacht Racing Union to co-ordinate and extend all these functions.

There are two alternative principles which may apply to the rules of class boats:

Enterprise          Designer: Jack Holt

Wayfarer          Designer: Ian Proctor
Photographer: Eileen Ramsay

Albacore          Designer : Fairey Marine Limited
Photographer : Vernon Stratton

Bosun          Designer: Ian Proctor
Photographer: Eileen Ramsay

1   One-design rules, which aim to produce each boat almost exactly the same as the next in hull shape, sail plan, weight and other matters affecting performance. In some cases these rules are extremely rigid, with very little variation allowed even in the placing of cleats and other small items of equipment; sometimes more variation in detail is permitted.

2   Restricted rules, which place limitations on certain aspects of design affecting performance. For instance, there are likely to be limits on overall length, minimum beam, minimum weight, maximum sail area, maximum height of sail plan, minimum amount of buoyancy apparatus. These would be better termed 'development rules', as the classes they control are free to undergo the evolutionary process of survival of the fittest and many designers are engaged competitively in producing them.

One-design classes have the advantage that the boats do not readily become outdated and production runs are longer and therefore the cost tends to be lower.

Most of the restricted classes in Britain are now developed to the stage at which design changes are less likely to produce dramatic differences in performance, so that they do not so quickly become outdated as hitherto. There is the added attraction in these restricted classes of greatly increased interest in the boats themselves, in which there may be much variation. This variation may, of course, make it relatively more difficult for the inexperienced to choose the right design for his purpose. Although the evolutionary process has slowed down in recent years, the keenest helmsmen in restricted classes are always seeking improvements and there is a regular supply of good second-hand boats at fairly low prices. These second-hand boats can often give a first class racing performance at really low cost.

A sound class organisation, spreading the class widely and ensuring adequate publicity, affects the cost of racing within the class. Because a large number of boats may be produced, many builders will probably be involved competitively and this naturally tends to keep the price down, though it may also lead to cheeseparing and lowering of building standards. Good class publicity also fosters the demand for secondhand boats and their resale value may be relatively high.

The popularity of a class often gives little indication of the virtues of the boat itself. It is natural that there should be more of the cheaper types than of the more expensive and sophisticated types. Though the cheapest boats may be quite adequate for the purpose for which they were designed, they may be no better value than their more expensive sisters, which are naturally less numerous. This follows the same pattern as cars or most other things. Quality has to be paid for, though efficient design and production can reduce costs.

# 6 Hull Design

The principles of sailing dinghy hull design are something of a mystery to most people who buy boats. Comparison of the behaviour and handling characteristics of different hulls may not enable them to be attributed to any particular design feature, except in the broadest terms. Obviously such a complex subject can only be touched on very lightly here.

The design of a sailing boat is inevitably a compromise seeking to achieve a wide range of performance and handling characteristics. Sometimes this compromise is more successful than at others, but at least an experienced designer should know what sort of dish will be produced from the ingredients he throws in the cooking pot and their proportions. He will continue to learn to his dying day, unless content to vegetate.

Apart from considerations of production costs, the objects in the design of the hull are:

1 Sufficient designed displacement to carry the intended load.
2 Speed under a wide range of conditions.
3 Stability and power to carry sufficient sail to give required performance.
4 Pleasant handling characteristics.
5 Seaworthiness and safety.

These objectives are not intended to be in order of priority, which may vary.

## a Displacement

Ever since Archimedes leapt from his bath crying 'Eureka', it has been fairly common knowledge that a body displaces its own weight of water. A boat, with all its gear and crew, has a total weight equal to the weight of water it displaces when floating. It is, therefore, easy to understand that if this weight has to be carried by a very small boat of, say 7' 6" in length at the waterline, this boat will have to be beamier and of greater draft than one carrying the same weight on a waterline of, say, 15 feet. It is obvious, therefore, that short boats tend to appear tubby and that length should add grace and speed to the lines. It must also be remembered that boats of all sizes are called upon to sail in much the same wave conditions, unless specialised or limited in their use. A 7' 6" dinghy will, therefore, have to be as capable of riding the same waves as a 15-footer and will, therefore, need as much depth of hull above the waterline (freeboard)—another factor adding to tubby appearance.

Careful design can, to some extent, mask the portliness of very short boats, but it is a snare and delusion to think that very small boats can perform properly and in safety unless there is adequate depth, beam and freeboard.

# b Resistance

Two main kinds of resistance to forward motion have to be overcome before a hull can move ahead. The first is known as wave-making resistance and the second is frictional resistance. At low speeds, the second retarding factor, due to skin friction, is far the more serious. Skin-friction of a hull at any given speed depends upon the condition and nature of its immersed surface and is directly proportional to the area of this immersed surface (wetted-surface area). This means that at any given speed and for any specific surface—for instance a smooth gel-coated GRP hull skin—skin friction is to all intents and purposes proportional to the wetted-surface area. So that, for light weather ability in particular, it is the aim of designers to reduce the wetted-surface area as much as is compatible with the length of the boat, the intended degree of stability and the power to resist the tendency to be blown to leeward.

Of all shapes, a circle has the shortest periphery relative to the area it encloses. In other words, a sphere of a given volume or displacement, has less wetted-surface area than any other shape. It might therefore seem that a hull with semi-circular underwater sections is ideal, but unfortunately there would be no inherent stability at all in a boat with such sections. A degree of stability of hull form is, of course, a necessity in all monohull sailing boats, though not essential in catamarans. Therefore, the concept of semi-circular underwater sections with their highly desirable minimum wetted-surface area, must be abandoned in favour of a compromise offering more stability.

Figures 18 and 19 show semi-circular and rectangular underwater hull sections of exactly the same area. That in figure 18 has the absolute minimum of wetted-surface area and no stability at all and that in figure 19 pays for almost maximum stability by having nearly maximum wetted-surface.

This is, of course, a great over-simplification of the problem. A single section, for example the midship section, has been considered. But a boat has a profile too, and to save wetted-area should this also be semi-circular? Yes it should, because the perfect shape to give least wetted-area for a given displacement is a sphere. Yet a sphere would not only be unstable in every direction, it would also create a great deal of wave-making resistance except at exceedingly low speeds.

To return to consideration of sections, however, and the battle between wetted-surface area and stability: the stability of a hull in action and its power to carry sail depends not on the underwater shape when at rest upright, but on the relationship of the centre of buoyancy of the hull in relation to the centre of gravity of the crew, hull, mast and gear and the forces of the wind on the sail. The weight of the crew plays a more important part still in the case of boats with trapeze or sliding seats, and a less important part in family sailing and cruising types.

# Load Carrying Proportions

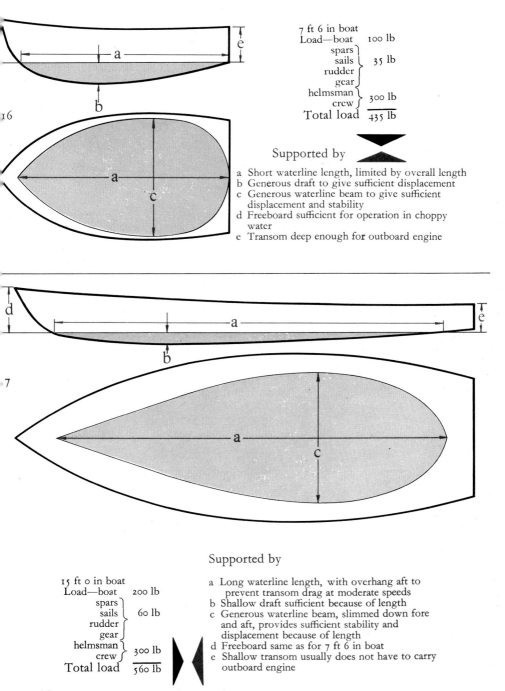

7 ft 6 in boat

| Load—boat | 100 lb |
|---|---|
| spars, sails, rudder, gear | 35 lb |
| helmsman, crew | 300 lb |
| **Total load** | **435 lb** |

## Supported by

a Short waterline length, limited by overall length
b Generous draft to give sufficient displacement
c Generous waterline beam to give sufficient displacement and stability
d Freeboard sufficient for operation in choppy water
e Transom deep enough for outboard engine

15 ft 0 in boat

| Load—boat | 200 lb |
|---|---|
| spars, sails, rudder, gear | 60 lb |
| helmsman, crew | 300 lb |
| **Total load** | **560 lb** |

## Supported by

a Long waterline length, with overhang aft to prevent transom drag at moderate speeds
b Shallow draft sufficient because of length
c Generous waterline beam, slimmed down fore and aft, provides sufficient stability and displacement because of length
d Freeboard same as for 7 ft 6 in boat
e Shallow transom usually does not have to carry outboard engine

Note: Although twice as long, the 15 footer has only to carry 29% more weight

Figure 20 shows a hull section of low stability at rest, but it is easy to see that it flares out to a wide beam at gunwale level and is able to support the crew's weight far outboard (to windward), and that as it heels the centre of buoyancy moves rapidly out from the centreline (to leeward), so that the centre of gravity of the whole ensemble and the centre of buoyancy of the hull are widely separated, creating a substantial righting moment. It gains stability as it heels, until it is very far over. Such a hull would have a low wetted-surface when fairly upright in light weather, but would have a big reserve of stability in a blow. The main snag to this form is that the gunwale reaches water level at much smaller angles of heel than with sections with more vertical topsides, so that cruising types need wider side decks. Also, if used with very slack bilges (easy curvature between the bottom and the topside) wetted-surface increases greatly on heeling.

On the other hand, the section in figure 21 though quite stable initially, loses stability rapidly as it approaches more extreme angles of heel. Such a hull would probably dull its crew into a false sense of security and then tip them in somewhat unexpectedly if they allowed the angle of heel to build up. It is therefore unsuitable for cruising or junior sailing.

The crew's ability to alter the attitude of the boat by moving his weight, makes it possible to reduce wetted-surface of some hull shapes in light airs by heeling to leeward. This is particularly useful to the relatively flat-bottomed, firm-bilged types.

The characteristics in hull shape which make for low wave-making resistance are much more complicated. From this point of view, the hull can best be considered in three parts:

1 The bow portion, or entry, which probably contributes relatively little to stability, but is concerned mainly with parting the water with as little resistance as possible, cleaving a way for the hull through waves without making it buck up and down like a hobby-horse, keeping down or turning away the spray from the bow wave without causing too much resistance, providing sufficient lift as the boat runs down a wave to prevent the bows driving under, and providing dynamic lift when the hull is moving fast, to help the boat to plane. Low wind resistance is important.

2 The midships portion or main body, which contributes most to weight-carrying displacement of water and stability.

3 The stern portion, or delivery, which generally contributes quite a lot to stability, but of which a most important function is to allow the water to close astern of the hull without undue drag and eddying. In any sailing boat the bottom of the transom should be clear of the water when the boat is at rest. Very slight immersion is permissible, but more than this causes eddying and drag. It is difficult to design a well tucked-up transom into a very small dinghy.

# Comparison of basic hull sections

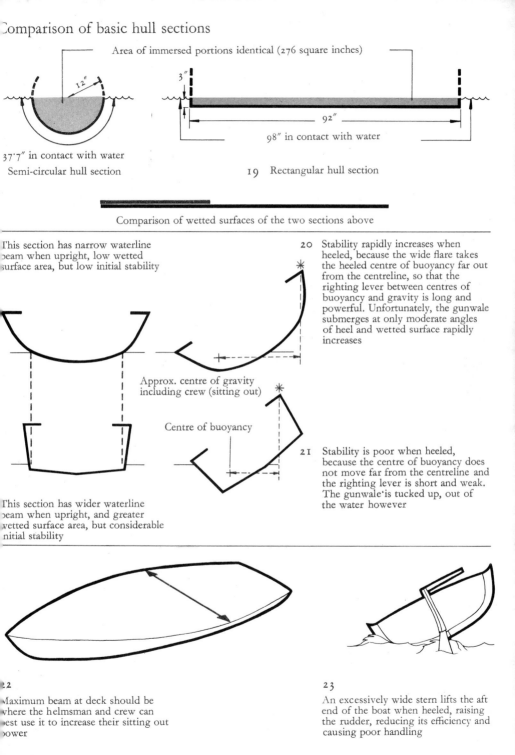

Area of immersed portions identical (276 square inches)

12"

3"

92"

98" in contact with water

37·7" in contact with water

Semi-circular hull section

19    Rectangular hull section

Comparison of wetted surfaces of the two sections above

This section has narrow waterline beam when upright, low wetted surface area, but low initial stability

20    Stability rapidly increases when heeled, because the wide flare takes the heeled centre of buoyancy far out from the centreline, so that the righting lever between centres of buoyancy and gravity is long and powerful. Unfortunately, the gunwale submerges at only moderate angles of heel and wetted surface rapidly increases

Approx. centre of gravity including crew (sitting out)

Centre of buoyancy

This section has wider waterline beam when upright, and greater wetted surface area, but considerable initial stability

21    Stability is poor when heeled, because the centre of buoyancy does not move far from the centreline and the righting lever is short and weak. The gunwale is tucked up, out of the water however

22

Maximum beam at deck should be where the helmsman and crew can best use it to increase their sitting out power

23

An excessively wide stern lifts the aft end of the boat when heeled, raising the rudder, reducing its efficiency and causing poor handling

25

Figure 24 shows a hull indicating some of the features thought to be desirable. It is important, both from the performance and good handling points of view, that the transition from a to c is gradually carried out through b.

In larger sailing boats, the designer has much more freedom in the evolution of the shape of the boat to give the necessary displacement. As the waterline length is greater, the draft and beam can be less, so that the curvature of the bottom and the waterlines are more gradual. As water does not like to be forced abruptly around corners or sharp curves, it offers far less resistance to a longer hull with more gradual curves for it to flow round.

## c Beam and balance

The maximum beam of a racing hull should always be where the helmsman and crew can use it to support their weight as far outboard as possible. Very wide sterns are sometimes justified in racing boats as normal developments of the lines, but they often contribute to poor handling characteristics and should be avoided in cruising types unless very carefully designed in relation to the bow sections, as they tend to lift the stern as the boat heels and lift the rudder partly out of the water, so that full control is lost.

A reasonably constant fore-and-aft balance of displacement at different angles of heel is something not usually considered very carefully in racing dinghy designs, but it makes a great deal of difference to controllability in heavy weather and is important in cruising and family boats.

A very small boat also tends to lack fore-and-aft stability and the bows must, therefore, be buoyant, otherwise when running before the wind they will bury and the boat may even be swamped by its own bow wave in fresh winds.

# 7 Decking and Layout

Almost every sailing boat over 10 feet in length has a foredeck. The notable exception is the International Fourteen Footer, which has had rules since 1927 prohibiting decks. Very small boats are usually completely undecked. Not only does a foredeck prevent some spray from the bow wave coming into the boat, it should also strengthen the structure, provide lateral support for the mast, help to spread the shroud loads, provide dry stowage for gear and neat stowage for buoyancy bags; or it can become a component of a forward buoyancy chamber. In addition, it helps to reduce wind resistance and can encourage the propulsive airstream into the jib.

The majority of sailing dinghies also have side decks, but in high

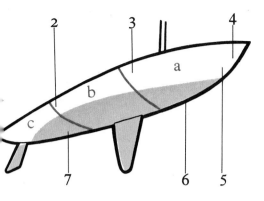

1 Stern of moderate width, to avoid lifting when heeled

2 Flare amidships increases sitting out power of crew

3 Flared topsides to deflect bow wave

4 Reasonably low freeboard to reduce windage

5 Fine, slicing bow for low resistance in waves

6 Reasonably deep chest, to reduce pounding in waves and provide dynamic lift for planing and buoyancy to avoid nosediving when running

7 Long, fairly flat run, allows hull to leave water cleanly, reducing drag at high speeds

| a Entry | b Main body | c Delivery |
|---|---|---|
| Introduces hull to water and waves. Provides dynamic lift for planing and buoyancy to resist depressing forces from sails when running before the wind | Provides most of the buoyancy and carrying power. Also main contributor to stability and sitting out power of crew | Guides waterflow lines so that the stern leaves the water cleanly, with little drag. Stern must be compatible with bow to avoid poor handling characteristics at high speeds, especially when heeled |

Toy                    Designer: Tony Allen    Lark                    Designer: Michael Jackson

performance boats this may be primarily to provide a comfortable perch for helmsman and crew, rather than to keep the water out, because an efficiently sailed boat avoids heeling far enough to ship water over the gunwale, except in the act of capsizing when side decks can do little to save it. When there are buoyancy tanks under the side decks, as in figure 25, side decks can prevent all but a little water coming aboard during a capsize. In some classes, the National Twelves for instance, in which side decks are optional and space at a premium, the modern trend is to do without them, thus increasing the range of movement of helmsman and crew and facilitating the movement of their weight. Gunwales should be wide, with generously curved edges for comfort. Often the gunwale is wider outside the boat than inside, in order to act as a spray deflector and to support the crew outboard as far as possible.

Aft decks are common and convenient for integral stern buoyancy, but less desirable since the introduction of flaps in the transom for rapid drainage. Transom flaps of course preclude aft buoyancy tanks. In many boats, the helmsman should have his weight well aft when reaching and running in fresh winds and the aft deck must allow this.

The centre thwart is an important structural member, tying the hull athwartships and bracing the centreboard case. It is, of course, also used as a seat for the crew and should be at a convenient height—high enough to enable the crew to move smoothly from it to the side deck or gunwale. As it somewhat protects self-bailers fitted in the bottom, it should be over the most advantageous site for these (usually the lowest part of the boat when in planing attitude), but it is important that the thwart does not bring the crew's weight too far aft when he sits on it.

Some dry stowage space is useful in almost any boat and should be provided for spinnakers, if carried. A net or lightweight polythene bin with drainage holes is excellent.

Sometimes floor boards are raised in cruising dinghies. This is a particular asset in boats with high freeboard, making sitting out easier and keeping feet dry. Raised floorboards add to the cost.

# 8 Buoyancy Apparatus

Any centreboard boat may capsize. None should ever be sailed without efficient buoyancy apparatus.

This apparatus may be divided into two main types; integral buoyancy in the form of tanks or chambers built into the structure of the boat; and separate tanks, bags or other units, secured to the boat.

## a Integral buoyancy

Integral buoyancy is usually preferable, because it can form part of the boat's structure and contribute to its strength. This is particularly so in GRP boats, in which transverse and longitudinal bulkheads are often desirable to overcome flexibility in the structure. Unfortunately it is sometimes difficult to make integral buoyancy tanks in GRP boats entirely watertight, particularly as the component bulkheads may be relatively heavily loaded and the joints between them and the hull heavily stressed. Great care needs to be taken in bonding components forming the buoyancy chamber and all boats having integral buoyancy should have a simple low pressure air test carried out on the buoyancy chambers by the builder. They should also, of course, all undergo a practical buoyancy test.

So far as possible, heavily stressed fittings should not be fastened to parts of the boat forming buoyancy chambers, but where this is unavoidable the fittings should be secured to generous reinforcing pads and through-fastenings (bolts or machine screws with washers and nuts) should be inserted with a mastic, so that there is little fear of the fitting working lose or leakage occurring through the hole for the fastenings.

Buoyancy chambers in wooden boats must be adequately ventilated through hatches or bungs. Hatches should be fitted with a suitable soft and compressible gasket, great care being taken to see that the gasket is unbroken and properly bonded at the corners and at other joints. The gasket shown in figure 30 is suitable, giving a narrow point of contact between the gasket and the surface on which it is closing, producing a watertight joint without too much pressure. A wide jointing area requires more pressure to overcome any unevenness and is therefore less satisfactory.

In spite of adequate design precautions and proper manufacture, hatches are always susceptible to leakage, sometimes brought on by poor maintenance. Hatches should, therefore, be positioned so that they are not submerged or only partially submerged during a capsize. This usually means they should be on the centreline and raised as far up as possible from the bottom of the hull.

Various fasteners are used for holding the hatches down. One highly effective type, in which the wedge principle applies pressure, is shown in figure 31. Toggle fasteners shown in figure 32 can be used when the hatch is mounted on the edge of a deck, and these apply firm pressure.

The covers of the smaller round plastic inspection hatches are usually secured by a quick-acting thread, which unfortunately does not always make a completely watertight joint. An 'O' ring or neoprene washer round the rim of such covers would be an improvement, but until some manufacturer recognises this, it is necessary to smear grease on them to keep them watertight.

A neoprene or rubber bung can be very effective if the hole to take it is accurately made to exactly the right size. This is shown in figure 33.

# b Separate buoyancy units

Separate buoyancy units are usually inflated bags. If properly manu-factured of tough material of adequate thickness, bags can give excellent service and have the advantage that any serious leakage is visible, as the bag deflates. The main source of trouble with buoyancy bags is that often they are ineffectively secured to the boat. The amount of lift they provide puts great strain on the fastenings securing them. This must always be taken into account. It is best to fasten them with Terylene webbing straps, secured under metal plates with stout screws into a strong structural member. There should be loops welded to the bags to prevent them slipping from the securing straps. It is embarrass-ing and dangerous to have buoyancy bags popping out of the boat in all directions during a capsize, but it quite frequently happens.

Occasionally buoyancy bags are used inside buoyancy chambers as a sort of second string, or when the buoyancy chamber leaks or is suspect. This is a bad practice, as there is a tendency to forget to inspect them for proper inflation.

All GRP boats with built-in air tanks should have additional buoyancy units to provide buoyancy if the buoyancy tanks become damaged in a collision because, unlike a wooden boat, the GRP structure will not float on its own. The most fool-proof form of buoyancy in this case is rigid polyurethane foam, which may be cut to shape from slabs or foamed in moulds. These foam units can be bonded into place within the buoyancy tanks and should provide sufficient buoyancy to float the boat in a completely waterlogged condition with the buoyancy tanks open and flooded, and supporting the normal crew of the boat, plus one. About 40 lbs positive buoyancy per person should be allowed in excess of that required to float the boat and all gear, including outboard engine if commonly used.

Polystyrene foam can also be used as buoyancy material, but is less satisfactory than polyurethane, because it is easily damaged, slightly water absorbent and cannot be bonded with normal resins used in GRP construction.

## c Disposition of buoyancy

Buoyancy apparatus has two main functions.

1 To provide lift to a waterlogged boat, floating her sufficiently high to support the crew in reasonable safety.

2 To facilitate righting and to keep the waterlogged boat in a practical state of equilibrium and stability.

Unfortunately these two functions conflict to some extent. Maximum lift in a waterlogged boat is most easily achieved by placing the buoyancy apparatus as low as possible in the boat, but this is likely to make the boat more difficult to right and keep righted. Figure 28 shows why. Conversely, relatively little lift may be given by buoyancy apparatus well placed for stability. For instance, if four buoyancy bags

**30**

Useful hatch gasket sections

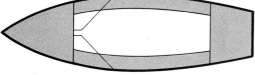

**5**

ntegral buoyancy. Tanks formed by
ongitudinal and transverse bulkheads

**31**

Simple hatch fastener, with wedge
action to compress gasket

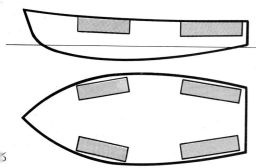

parate buoyancy units. Inflated bags or
bs of foam buoyancy material

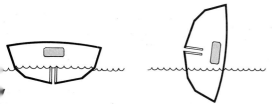

**32**

Toggle hatch fastener, clamps
hatch firmly to compress gasket

uoyancy should be sufficient to float waterlogged
at high enough to drain to level of top of centre-
ard case. Hatches should be clear of undrained
ter when boat is level or on her side

**33**

Rubber or neoprene bung

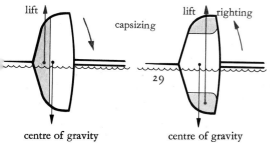

lift — capsizing — lift — righting

**29**

centre of gravity — centre of gravity

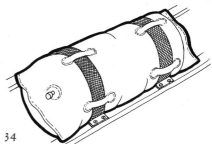

**34**

Buoyancy bag secured by straps

are positioned as shown in figure 26 the boat will be very stable and safe, but will lie low in the water when swamped.

Undoubtedly the safest boat is one which, in a water-logged condition, is a stable raft, supporting the crew until they are rescued or are able to get ashore or bail out. Another advantage of this characteristic is that the boat floats low in the water, making it far easier for the crew to clamber on board again.

Most of the flat-out racing fraternity want to be able to right the boat after a capsize and continue sailing with the least possible delay. This demands a large amount of buoyancy, usually provided by one buoyancy chamber forward and another aft, with smaller side tanks or bags arranged reasonably high in the hull, to provide lateral stability and help in righting the boat. This layout is shown in figure 25 and gives maximum fore and aft stability as well as stability athwartships. Sometimes the aft buoyancy unit is omitted and larger side tanks are provided so that the boat can drain through flaps in the transom.

It is stressed again that practical buoyancy tests and regular inspection of buoyancy apparatus are essential safeguards.

## d Personal buoyancy

Although not within the scope of this book, personal buoyancy must be mentioned as a safety aid. There are many types of buoyancy jacket on the market. Always wear one in rough or cold weather, and preferably whenever sailing. Children should never go afloat without one. It is only too easy to become separated from a capsized boat, which drifts away very quickly if it is floating high and in a fresh wind. In cold water strength is quickly sapped and a considerable amount of energy is usually required to right a boat and get back on board.

# 9 Rudders and Tillers

## a Lifting or fixed?

Rudders of centreboard boats can always be removed from the fittings on the stern; the only exception is in International Canoes where the rudder pivots in a removable framework forward of the stern. As the rudder blade normally extends about 18 inches below the waterline it cannot be used in its normal position in shallow water, yet good directional control is highly desirable when leaving or coming into a shore crowded with other boats trying to do the same thing.

Rudders are, therefore, of two main types:

1 Lifting rudders, with the blade pivoted in the stock or framework, which pivots vertically on the stern of the boat. This permits the rudder assembly to be positioned on the transom, together with the tiller, and the boat can be steered reasonably efficiently even in very shallow water. When the water is deep enough, the blade is lowered. The blade may

## Heavy weather

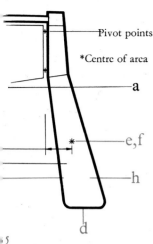

## B  Light weather

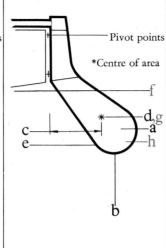

## C  All weather compromise

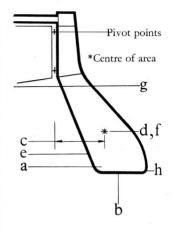

### Advantages

a  Narrow blade at waterline reduces sucking down of air at high speeds, which destroys clean flow

b  Deep blade operates in undisturbed water, giving good steering effect at high speeds

c  Narrow blade, with centre of area nearly vertical below pivot points, reduces load on the tiller and lifting action on the stern when boat is heeled

### Disadvantages

d  Vigorous helm action at high speeds causes greater capsizing leverage because of depth

e  Because of c, little 'feel' on the helm in light airs

f  Because of c, very difficult to 'flick' the stern round or turn quickly in very light airs

g  Near-vertical leading edge picks up weed and flotsam

h  Large wetted surface area causes frictional resistance

### Advantages

a  Small wetted surface area causes little frictional resistance in light airs

b  Shallow blade produces little capsizing leverage during vigorous helm action

c  Centre of area well aft of pivot points gives plenty of 'feel' on the helm in light airs

d  Because of c, easy to 'flick' stern round or turn quickly in very light airs

e  Raked leading edge does not pick up weed and flotsam easily

### Disadvantages

f  Blade must be wider at waterline and tends to suck down air

g  Because of c, heavy load on helm at high speeds

h  Because of c, acts as elevator lifting stern when boat is heeled

### Advantages

a  Fairly small wetted surface area

b  Moderate depth produces only moderate capsizing leverage

c  Centre of area far enough aft to give 'feel', but not sufficiently far aft to cause elevator action when boat heels

d  Because of c, fairly easy to 'flick' stern round or turn quickly in light airs

e  Raked leading edge does not collect weed or flotsam seriously

f  Because of c, only moderate load on helm in heavy weather

g  Moderate width at waterline reduces sucking down of air

h  Clean break away of flow from tip reduces drag

### Disadvantages

i  More wetted surface area than B

j  Being a compromise has the advantages of A and B but in smaller measure

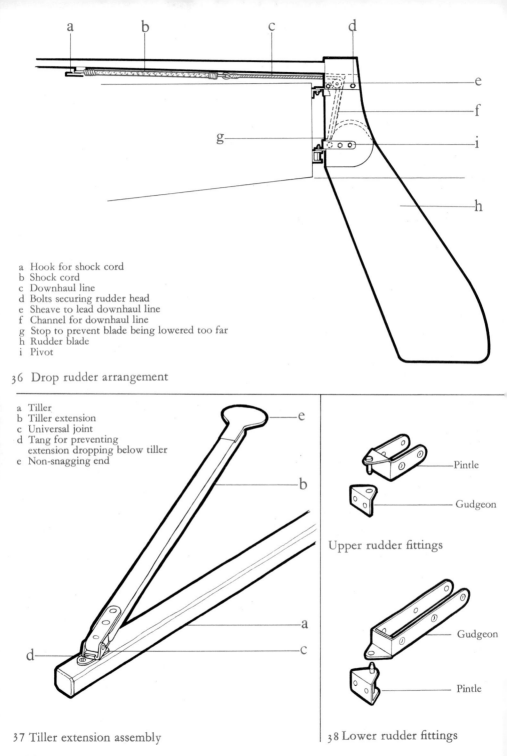

a  Hook for shock cord
b  Shock cord
c  Downhaul line
d  Bolts securing rudder head
e  Sheave to lead downhaul line
f  Channel for downhaul line
g  Stop to prevent blade being lowered too far
h  Rudder blade
i  Pivot

36  Drop rudder arrangement

a  Tiller
b  Tiller extension
c  Universal joint
d  Tang for preventing
   extension dropping below tiller
e  Non-snagging end

Pintle

Gudgeon

Upper rudder fittings

Gudgeon

Pintle

37 Tiller extension assembly

38 Lower rudder fittings

be of metal or other unbuoyant material and may drop down under its own weight, the blade being lifted by a line running through a lead at the top of the rudder stock and along the tiller to a cleat. Alternatively, and more commonly, the blade is buoyant and floats up, being pulled down by a cord running within the rudder stock through a lead at the top of the stock and along the tiller to a cleat. Sometimes shockcord elastic is incorporated in the downhaul, so, if the blade hits an underwater object, it recoils from the impact. Though slightly more expensive the advantages of lifting rudders are obvious. Not only is there proper control when sailing off a shallow shore, but often when racing, or even cruising, it is desirable to sail into shallow water to avoid adverse currents, to cut a corner, or simply because the tide has dropped. The disadvantages are that the slightly more complicated arrangement is susceptible to minor troubles. The blade may be sloppy in the stock, causing lack of positive feel and response through the helm, which makes steering difficult in rough water and certainly is inefficient in a racing boat. The downhaul or lifting lines may deteriorate and break.

Obviously, the rudder blade must be strong, both when fully lowered and in the raised positions. In all positions the rudder stock should give the blade adequate support and there should be a sufficient area of blade within the stock to permit this. The blade itself should also be stiff, as flexibility makes steering very difficult. Glassfibre blades are sometimes used but frequently are too flexible, yet if sufficiently stiff are excellent, because they do not shrink and swell, so that the blade can be held quite closely by the stock without fear of it jamming.

2 Fixed rudders have the blade in a fixed position in the stock. This necessitates removing the rudder from the stern and holding it rather like a paddle when steering with it in shallow water. While the helmsman is pre-occupied in fitting the rudder on to the stern, he cannot see where he is going and in fresh winds control is difficult.

## b Rudder construction

The rudder blade should have at least some semblance of streamline form, the simplest being a bevel on the leading and trailing edges. If the bottom of the blade is more or less horizontal, it is not important to bevel this and it may be desirable to leave it flat, making it less easily damaged. More expensive rudder blades may be protected by metal bands on the leading and bottom edges.

The rudder head, into which the tiller fits, should be very strong and held to the stock by through-rivets or bolts. Ordinary wood-screw fastenings are inadequate.

Rudder hangings in all but the very smallest boats should be of stainless steel. There is considerable strain on them and light alloy castings are usually inadequate except for sailing in very smooth and calm water.

## c Tillers

The tiller should be of sufficient sectional dimensions to give a positive connection between the helmsman and the rudder. More than very slight flexibility in the tiller is undesirable. In particular the tiller should be strong at its junction with the rudder head and on no account should there be reduction in dimensions at this point. The best material for tillers is oak.

All racing boats have pivoted tiller extensions, to enable the helmsman to steer when sitting out. The joint between the extension and the tiller must be strong and ordinary bolts are normally unsatisfactory, as they may tighten when the extension is swivelled and make it impossible to move the joint. The extension should have something to grip near its outer end, and preferably this should be shaped so that it cannot catch on the helmsman's clothing. Tiller extensions have been known to get stuck up his sleeve at a crucial moment.

# 10 Centreboards, Centreplates

Unless really heavy, the centreboard or centreplate contributes very little to stability. Twenty years ago some centreboards had lead tips to concentrate the weight at the bottom, but these were comparatively expensive. In high performance racing boats it is now accepted that considerations of stability provided by heavy centreplates are over-ridden by the desirability of saving weight to improve planing performance.

## a Lateral resistance

Most people who read this book will know that when a boat sails to windward she does so at an angle of about 45° to the wind, although the speed of the boat itself reduces the effective angle of the wind to the boat to about 35°, sometimes less. In its action on the sails, the wind produces a force which can be resolved into a forward component and a sideways or lateral component. The forward component produces forward movement in the boat, but the lateral component would push the boat sideways, if it were not for the underwater shape of the boat resisting this sideways thrust and for the additional resistance contributed by the centreboard, centreplate or daggerboard. This is called 'lateral resistance'.

## b The best shape

Centreboards and related devices to provide lateral resistance also have other effects on performance. They considerably increase the wetted-surface area of the hull without adding appreciably to the displacement, so that they increase the frictional resistance. If insufficiently heavy to act as ballast, they actually add to the capsizing forces on the boat when sailing to windward, as figure 1 shows. Therefore, though the centreboard is essential to provide lateral resistance, it should not be bigger than necessary to perform this function efficiently, extra area adding to frictional resistance and increased depth adding to the heeling leverage.

Opinions differ on the best shape for centreboards. The leading edge and area immediately aft of this is the most effective portion in providing lateral resistance, so there is some virtue in making it deep and relatively narrow, but this increases the heeling leverage. Additionally, in rough water, deep centreboards may increase resistance and detract from good handling characteristics, because the hull is influenced by the water which is in motion near the wave's surface, while the lower end of the centreboard is influenced by water which is moving less fast or not at all three or four feet down below the surface (it is a characteristic of waves that water particles are in motion on the surface, but not more deeply). To combat these considerations, the centreboard may best be tapered towards its lower end, with more area close to the hull. Centreboards may frequently hit the mud, and shapes permitting easy turning and release when this happens are desirable. To achieve this the tip of the blade should be narrow, tapering from the leading edge and preferably rounded.

Centreboards should be of approximately streamline section or at least with bevelled edges, and in the case of pivoting centreboards, the bottom should also be bevelled, otherwise there will be drag and turbulence when it is partially raised.

## c  Boards, plates or daggerboards

There are three main devices to provide lateral resistance.

### 1 Centreboards

Boards pivoted on a pin through a centreboard case. When lowered, the tip of the board moves forward. Thus the centre of lateral resistance (which to simplify matters may be taken as the centre of its area) moves forward. This moving of the centre of lateral resistance (CLR) is a great advantage, as in strong winds it is desirable to move the CLR slightly aft, and when reaching with the wind abeam the centre should be moved further aft again, while when running with the wind aft the centreboard may be swung even further aft or raised altogether to save frictional resistance.

Wooden centreboards float up on their own unless held down in some way. Commonly a friction pad is fitted to the board to act on the inside faces of the centreboard case, as shown in figure 40. The friction may be increased by tightening the screws securing the friction tube and spreading it so that it exerts more pressure on the inside of the centreboard case. There are two main snags to this method. First, and particularly in GRP boats, centreboard cases are usually stiffer at top and bottom, where they are reinforced, so the frictional resistance is greater when the board is right up or right down, and may be insufficient in between, where the centreboard case can flex. Secondly,

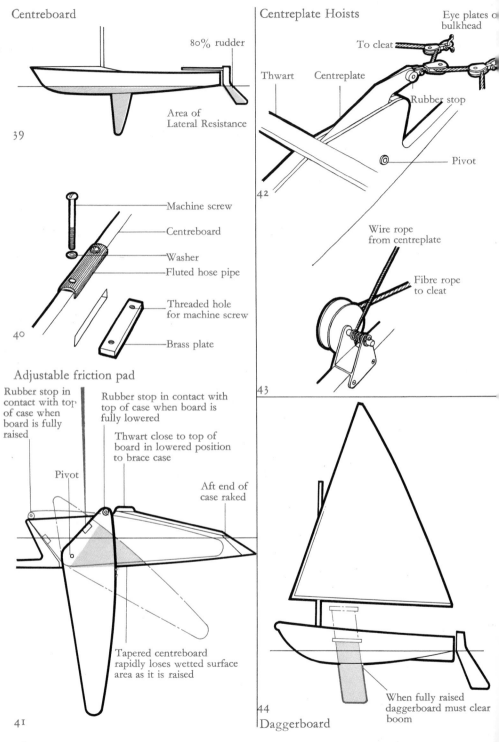

Centreboard

80% rudder

Area of
Lateral Resistance

39

Machine screw

Centreboard

Washer
Fluted hose pipe

Threaded hole
for machine screw

Brass plate

40

Adjustable friction pad

Rubber stop in
contact with top
of case when
board is fully
raised

Rubber stop in contact with
top of case when board is
fully lowered

Thwart close to top of
board in lowered position
to brace case

Pivot

Aft end of
case raked

Tapered centreboard
rapidly loses wetted surface
area as it is raised

41

Centreplate Hoists

Eye plates o
bulkhead

To cleat

Thwart    Centreplate

Rubber stop

Pivot

42

Wire rope
from centreplate

Fibre rope
to cleat

43

When fully raised
daggerboard must clear
boom

44
Daggerboard

it is only possible to adjust the friction device when the board is down, and this means doing it when the boat is afloat, or perhaps rolling the boat on its side ashore. This is not always convenient.

A better arrangement, but more expensive, is two friction devices fitted to the top of the centreboard case in contact with each side of the centreboard. This avoids variations in the applied friction and the device can be adjusted more readily.

### 2 Centreplates

Simply metal centreboards. No frictional devices are required, as their own weight keeps them down. Centreplates are raised by a tackle attached to the upper forward corner, which may be extended forward as an arm to increase leverage. This tackle can conveniently lead to each side of the hull so the plate can be hoisted from either side while sailing. The arrangement shown in figure 42 gives the mechanical advantage of 2—1. Occasionally a very heavy centreplate is hoisted by a wire to a drum and spindle winch, the relative diameters of spindle and drum providing the mechanical advantage. Heavy centreplates, though justified in some cruising boats as an aid to stability, are not much used these days, and need careful handling, for if allowed to go down with a bang they may damage the boat or the crew.

### 3 Daggerboards

The simplest means of providing lateral resistance. They slide up and down in a short casing and cannot be swung fore and aft to any great extent. They are justifiable when simplicity and economy are important. They have the disadvantages of being unable to move the centre of lateral resistance and of projecting upwards when raised, often to the extent of getting in the way of the boom—a nuisance when in shallow water. If carefully designed, the top should just clear the boom when the lower edge is level with the bottom of the boat, but if there is a kicking strap, this will nearly always foul a raised daggerboard.

The daggerboard may be held in raised position by a pin passing through the board, or by shock cord engaging with a notch on the edge of the board.

Another disadvantage is that it is much more difficult to raise the dagger board if the boat goes aground and the board may tend to jam in the casing in these circumstances.

# 11 Rigs

## a Una

Una rig—a single mainsail—is generally used only for single-handed boats. Though quite efficient—and in very restricted water, such as the narrow rivers, possibly even more efficient than sloop rig because of its extreme simplicity in handling—it tends to be rather boring when there is more than one person in the boat, as the crew has no sail to handle.

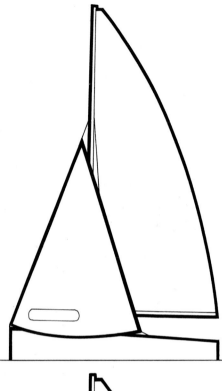

## Long-footed, low jib

45

### Advantages

1 Extra sail area low down, where it does not add much to heeling forces
2 Closes gap between jib and hull, reducing eddying under foot of jib

### Disadvantages

1 Harder to tack quickly, as jib and sheets have to b eased past shrouds
2 More sheet to handle
3 Visibility much reduced. Transparent plastic window essential. Added expense
4 Relationship between jib and mainsail critical, as jib tends to deflect wind on to lee side of mainsail. Leads to expense in obtaining really efficient sails

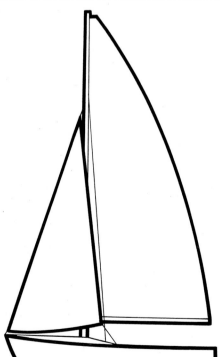

## Short-footed jib

46

### Advantages

1 Easier to tack quickly. Usually sheeted inside shrouds, so sheets do not have to be eased past rigging
2 Sail area raised into stronger wind stream
3 Foor of jib raised clear of disturbance to wind stream caused by hull
4 Visibility quite good. Plastic window not essentia
5 Relationship between jib and mainsail not quite s critical. Easier to make sails operate efficiently
6 Much more suitable for junior crews

## b Sloop

Sloop rig—mainsail and jib, sometimes supplemented by a spinnaker—is used almost universally for centreboard sailing boats with the exception of single handers. Jibs are of two general types:

1 Short footed, probably extending no further aft than the shrouds supporting the mast.

2 Genoa jibs, overlapping the mainsail to a considerable extent and well aft of the shrouds.

Genoa jibs have evolved mainly as a result of rules in certain classes, which permit portions of the sail area to be carried 'free' without inclusion in the maximum measured sail area allowed. A rig with a Genoa can seldom be as efficient as one with a similar area using a shorter footed jib.

## c Bermuda and other rigs

Bermuda rig is almost universal for racing boats. It is simple, light, has low wind resistance and is cheap. Bermuda sails are easy to make. The most common alternative to Bermuda rig is gunter. The gunter gaff or yard is virtually an extension of the mast. Preferably, the lower end of the yard is held to the mast by a swivelling slide running on a track on the mast; the track can then also be used for sail slides. Alternatively the yard is held by some form of jaw to the mast, when sail slides cannot be used. The yard, with sail attached, is hoisted by a halyard running from about one-third of the way up the yard through a sheave at the top of the mast. This means that the yard must overlap the mast by about one-third of its length and this, of course, adds weight and windage aloft.

Gunter rig is particularly useful:

1 If a small dinghy is kept on exposed moorings, the shorter mast reducing windage and making capsizing unlikely.

2 If the boat is used as a yacht's tender or carried on top of a car, the spars can probably be stowed within it. Some boats with this rig specially provide for internal spar stowage.

Spar stowage within the boat is no longer impossible with Bermuda rig, jointed metal masts now being available which are almost indistinguishable from one-piece masts.

Children's boats sometimes have sail plans designed specifically to reduce the height of the centre of effort of the sails, as an aid to stability. These rigs are normally a variant of gunter, lug or lateen rig. The stability objective is obviously desirable in junior classes, but usually it is more difficult for a child to hoist a sail with a gaff or yard compared with the simplicity of hoisting a Bermuda mainsail.

## d Sail area

Sails are, of course, the means of converting wind force into driving

## Gunter

47

### Advantages

a  Nearly as efficient a shape as Bermuda rig
b  All spars are short and can easily be stowed in the boat
c  Little windage on low mast. Makes capsize on exposed moorings unlikely. Suitable for yachts' tenders
d  Yard reefs with mainsail, reducing height of centre of gravity and capsizing leverage
e  Short mast is easily stepped by children or when boat is afloat (important for yachts' tenders)
f  Easy to row or paddle with sail lowered

### Disadvantages

g  Weight of spars greater than Bermuda rig
h  Yard swings about while sail is being hoisted—difficult for young children
i  Movement between yard and mast makes efficient setting of mainsail more difficult

## Spritsail

48

### Advantages

a  All spars are short and stowable within boat
b  Centre of area of sail plan is low, reducing capsizing leverage
c  Short mast is easily stepped

### Disadvantages

d  Sail shape inefficient and performance poor
e  The centre of sail area is very far aft, making it necessary to balance this with a bigger dagger board or centreboard inconveniently far aft
f  The sprit or yard interferes with the wind flow across the sail

## Lateen

49

### Advantages

a  Short mast. Joint in yard can permit all spars to stow within boat
b  Very simple to rig
c  Centre of sail area fairly low
d  Area of sail ahead of mast helps to bring bows round when tacking

### Disadvantages

e  Heavier total spar weight than Bermuda
f  Mast interferes with air flow across sail
g  Cannot be reefed

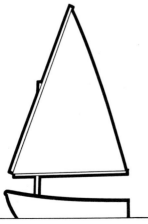

power. Given equal efficiency of design, the more sail area, the greater the power—and hence higher potential speed.

In producing the forward driving component from the wind stream, a strong lateral component is also produced, trying to push the sails (and hence the mast and the boat) sideways. Obviously, this force is tending to capsize the boat and in consequence greater sail area demands either:

1  Greater stability in hull form, by means of beam and configuration, or

2  Greater crew weight or increased leverage for the crew's weight by getting this further outboard, or

3  A combination of both.

Increasing the beam and stability of the hull almost inevitably puts up the wetted-surface area, and consequently tends to slow the boat in light weather, to some extent nullifying the effect of increasing sail area. Putting more emphasis on the disposition of the weight of the crew as a stabilising factor calls for greater skill, agility and energy on the part of the crew.

The capsizing forces derived from the sails can be reduced by lowering the height of the sail plan, but this tends to decrease efficiency for a given sail area, as most of the drive to windward comes from the forward one-third of the sail. Mainsails with comparatively long booms badly unbalance the sail plan when the mainsail is freed off for reaching or running and may give rise to difficult handling characteristics in fresh winds, such as extreme weather helm and broaching.

There is, therefore, a practical limit to the amount of sail area suitable for a particular type and size of hull and the type of crew likely to sail it. A jib area of about 30 square feet is usually the maximum that a girl can manage.

## e  Spinnakers

When reaching and running there is, of course, less heeling force acting upon the sail plan in proportion to the driving force. The hull is driven considerably faster, which may bring its own stability and handling problems, but will also be better able to carry greater sail area. Additional sail area can be provided by a spinnaker.

There are several different types of spinnaker, some of which, like Genoa jibs, have evolved as a result of trying to squeeze the maximum sail area from a rule framework. These rule-exploiting sails are sometimes relatively inefficient for their area and often can be used effectively only through a limited range of wind directions, smaller more efficiently shaped spinnakers being substituted as the need arises.

Other more enlightened class rules encourage more versatile spinnakers which can be used through a large range of wind directions, obviating the need for a number of alternative sails. A modern spherical-cut spinnaker of the right proportions can be used quite close to the wind,

Extruded aluminium alloy; watertight; buoyant. Halyards contained aft of web. Low wind resistance. Clean wind flow from mast to sail.

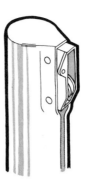

Aluminium alloy masthead fitting. The sheave cage, riveted in aft of the web, is fitted with a reinforced plastic sheave which leads the halyard down in the track portion of the mast. There is an eye for the burgee halyard. The cap is welded to seal the mast tube.

Extruded aluminium alloy aft, with formed plate bonded to it. Foamed polystyrene buoyancy. Wind flow disturbed by rib at side.

Hollow, laminated wood. Self buoyant. Shoulder at aft edge disturbs air flow on to sail.

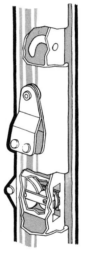

Stainless steel tangs for shrouds and trapeze attachment, carried on tubular rivet through light alloy mast. The spinnaker halyard is led through the curved tube above.

The jib halyard is taken through the mast by two sheaves; the forward sheave is of large diameter to reduce the bending strains on the halyard, the aft sheave is smaller to reduce the overall size of the sheave cage. Weight and windage is very low.

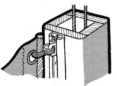

Box section wood. Metal track for sail slides. Self buoyant. Poor air flow on to sail. Easy for amateur construction.

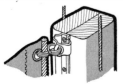

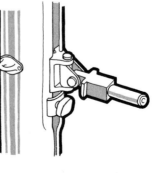

This type of stainless steel goose-neck slides in the track of an aluminium alloy mast and can be clamped at varying heights.

To reef, the boom is pushed aft then rotated on the round section of the pin, rolling the sail on to the boom, which is then prevented from unrolling by the engagement of the square shoulder. A side spinnaker boom eye is shown.

Solid wood, laminated. Metal track for sail slides. External halyards. Poor air flow on to sail. Heavy. Cheap.

sometimes even when the wind is forward of the beam, adding considerably to the interest in using this sail skilfully.

Another factor in spinnaker efficiency is the length of the pole from which the spinnaker is set and which assists in spreading the sail and keeping it clear of the mainsail and jib. One end of the spinnaker pole is attached to the tack of the sail and the other end is attached to the mast. Some class rules force spinnaker poles to be very short in relation to the size of sail set from them, with consequent inefficiency. Extremely long poles are difficult to stow in the boat and difficult to use, and a happy medium is desirable.

Spinnakers add to expense and complication, and call for a fair degree of skill from both helmsman and crew, so may be thought unsuitable for beginners. In a relatively heavy boat, even a quite large spinnaker may have a disappointing effect on performance, particularly if not handled very well, but with lighter types of boat, which plane more readily, the additional drive from a spinnaker may permit planing at much lower wind speeds and, for this reason in particular, a spinnaker may considerably improve performance, becoming a vital race-winning factor. This being the case, it must be decided whether the additional skill called for in properly handling the spinnaker will be welcomed as an added interest and excitement in sailing, or will be less welcome as a further complication and expense.

# 12 Masts and Spars

At present there are two principal alternative materials for the construction of masts, booms and spinnaker poles. Aluminium alloy has now almost completely superseded wood, and virtually every new type of boat which is designed uses spars of this material. But wood is still used in some older classes which still prohibit aluminium alloy on the grounds that metal masts may give a performance advantage, which would be a digression from some strict one-design principles. GRP masts have also been made—a few in this country, but more in Sweden, France and Holland—but the properties of the material show no advantages over aluminium alloy, the relationship between strength, flexibility and weight of a light alloy mast being preferable, and its manufacture easier and less expensive.

Solid wooden masts are now only used in very small, cheap dinghies, and are usually of spruce, laminated of two or three pieces to avoid warping or twisting. The more common wooden mast is hollow, built up of two pieces, often pear-shaped in section with an integral groove to take the mainsail bolt rope, but sometimes rectangular with a track screwed to it. The only really satisfactory material for a wooden mast is sitka spruce, which is becoming increasingly difficult to obtain in good quality.

There are three main forms of construction for metal masts. The least commonly used is a round or oval tube with a specially extruded track section riveted to it. The tube is usually untapered.

Another type of metal mast is formed from two main components, one being an extrusion of the after part of the mast section—including a track to carry the edge of the sail—and the other being an extrusion or formed shape of the forward part of the mast. The two components are bonded together with a metal-to-metal adhesive, there being a lip at the joint to reinforce it. Tapering is accomplished by removing material from the edges of the forward component of the section and reforming the shape to meet the aft component. This type of mast is usually filled with polystyrene foam buoyancy material.

The most common type of aluminium alloy mast is formed from a single extrusion, usually pear-shaped with a groove on the aft side, which is divided from the main tube by a web. The space between the web and the groove to take the sail is sufficient to take the running rigging (halyards). These masts are usually tapered by removing an elongated 'V' from the foreside of the tube, reforming the shape of the remainder to bring the cut edges together, and rewelding. This type of mast is usually anodised, giving further protection against corrosion and almost eliminating the need for maintenance. The leads for jib or spinnaker halyards, which have to pass from the foreside of the tube to the aft side, are taken through welded channels, so that the main tubular part of the section, which is sealed at top and bottom, is designed to be watertight and buoyant. This is probably the ideal way of making a metal mast buoyant, as the lightweight buoyant materials which are sometimes used, such as polystyrene foam, retain moisture within the mast tube, causing added weight and corrosion.

Cheaper quality masts may use light alloy die castings for some fittings, but those for high performance boats normally use stainless steel fittings attached with rivets, bolts or self tapping screws. Stainless fittings should be bedded in zinc chromate paste to eliminate electrolytic corrosion between the stainless steel and light alloy.

The fittings available for modern spars range from basic items whose function is standard to all types of mast and includes such things as shroud tangs and halyard sheaves, to items varying considerably between different types of mast, such as goosenecks, connecting the boom to the mast. The materials and design of these fittings affect their cost and efficiency, stainless steel and the tougher reinforced plastics being far preferable to die-cast light alloys and nylon in most instances, though usually a little more expensive. It depends, of course, on the size and power of the boat whether the cheaper type of fitting is adequate.

It may be emphasised here that the prime function of spars is, of course, to support and spread the sails in the most efficient manner, with the least possible interference to the functioning of the sails themselves by wind resistance or disturbance of the air flow across them, and with the minimal addition of weight aloft compatible with the strength and ability of the spars to support the sails in all reasonable conditions.

## a Flexibility of spars

The camber or horizontal curvature of sails should vary according to the wind strength, to get the maximum drive from the sails under varying conditions. This is a complicated subject but, to put it very briefly, more curvature is desirable in light winds than in fresh winds, when heavily cambered sails produce a strong heeling force, making the boat difficult to hold upright. Ideally, also, the mainsail should have more camber in it when the boat is reaching and running than when it is close hauled.

The camber or fullness is produced by the sailmaker, mainly by convex-curving the edges of the sail. When these curved edges are set on straight spars, the extra material in the curved portion of the sail goes towards producing the camber. If the tension on the edges of the sail is slackened, this also allows more camber into the sail, though it also reduces its spread. The control of this tension will be described later.

As just mentioned, the curvature on the edges of the sails produces camber if they are set in straight spars. But, if these spars are themselves curved, the sail will be pulled out flat again. The camber of the sail can therefore be decreased by bending the spars.

Much development has taken place in the past ten years to evolve efficient flexible rigs, which more or less automatically control the camber of the mainsail. The forces acting on the mast are shown in figure 53. The head of the mast is pulled aft by the tension through the leech of the mainsail. Tension on the mainsheet and through the kicking strap causes forward thrust from the boom at the gooseneck, also tending to bend the mast. The heavy compression loads in the mast below the hounds (attachment of shrouds and forestay) reinforce the bending loads from the masthead and gooseneck and increase the bend below the hounds. All this can be seen in the diagram.

The greater the tension on the mainsheet, the more the mast will bend, and increasing loads on the leech of the sail in heavier winds will also cause more mast bend. Therefore, in strong winds, when the sheeting loads are heaviest, mast bend will be greatest and the sail will be flattened most—which is just what is wanted.

Some flattening action can also be produced by bending the boom, and this is most easily achieved by attaching the mainsheet near the middle of the boom, rather than at its end. If this centre mainsheet system is adopted, the attachment of the mainsheet blocks to the boom can be by slides running in a track on the underside of the boom, so that the sheet can be moved aft in strong winds to produce more forward thrust through the boom to the mast, causing the mast to bend more. In light airs the attachment points can be moved forward,

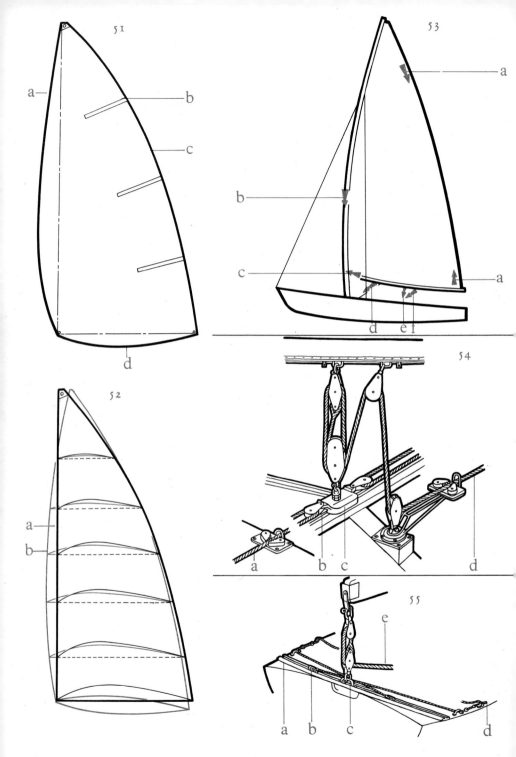

decreasing the thrust on the mast and reducing mast bend.

With a centre mainsheet arrangement, similar to that shown in figure 54, the boom can be strapped down hard to tension the mainsail leech and produce forward boom thrust, but the sail can still be eased out or trimmed in by means of the lines controlling the position of the traveller sliding on its track, which is mounted on the boat. This is less readily achieved when the mainsheet is attached to the end of the boom, as the horizontal trim of the mainsail is then controlled by the mainsheet alone, so that easing the boom out also allows it to rise, permitting the mainsail leech to slacken and the sail to twist, also losing some control over the bend in the topmast.

It is essential that the mainsheet traveller used with centre mainsheet systems should move easily even when under the very heavy loads imposed, otherwise proper control is lost and frequent capsizes result. There are several special travellers available, one of which is illustrated. Centre mainsheet systems are generally considered unsuitable for boats under 14 feet, because sufficiently quick trimming of the mainsail is difficult. In these cases, wide and adjustable mainsheet horses at the stern permit the mainsail to be eased out, but at the same time pulled down hard in much the same way as with centre mainsheet systems, but over a more limited range.

To give the correct bending characteristics, the spars must, of course, be properly designed to achieve this. It is important that the relationship between the length of the mast above the hounds and the length below is correct, though class rules may in some cases make this

49

impossible. A very short topmast has insufficient leverage to permit it to exert its influence on the part of the mast below the hounds. Too long a topmast tends to absorb too much of the bend induced by tension in the leech of the sail and does not transmit it effectively to the lower part of the mast, where curvature is usually most needed.

Wooden masts may be used for flexible rigs and can be quite successful, but the heavy compression loads to which they are subjected when at full bend are very liable to cause breakage. Metal masts stand these strains much more readily.

## b Sail control fittings

Modern sails are made of low stretch material, such as Terylene or the American Dacron. The fabric of the mainsail is attached to bolt ropes, either by sewing directly to the ropes or by enveloping them with the material like a sleeve. There is some elasticity in the bolt ropes (they may even be shock cord) and they are tensioned while the fabric is being attached to them, so that less tension on the bolt ropes bunches up the fabric slightly along its roped edges, causing it to become more 'baggy' (fuller)—but slightly smaller. Control of tension on the edges is therefore important in controlling the camber of sails. There are many different gadgets to assist in altering tension on the edges of sails, some of them quite sophisticated and remote controlled, so that operation is quick and effective.

The tension in the luff of the mainsail may be controlled in three different ways. The simplest is by hoisting the head of the sail to the same position each time and cleating or locking the halyard to hold it there, the foot of the sail then being adjusted in height by means of a sliding gooseneck, which can be moved up and down to alter the position of the boom, then locked. An alternative method is by means of a ratchet winch for the halyard, but this method is more expensive, less efficient and now seldom used.

The third and best method of controlling edge tension, often used in conjunction with a sliding gooseneck, is the Cunningham hole system. In this there is a hole or cringle in the sail about 12 inches above the gooseneck, and a line attached at one end to the boom is passed through this hole round a sheave (to give additional purchase), through the hole again and finally to a cleat. This method has the advantage that the sail is spread to its maximum area when the tension on the luff is eased in light weather (when as much sail area as possible is needed); when the tension has to be increased, this can be done by means of the line going through the Cunningham hole, without altering the sail area, though it does somewhat bunch the sail at the lower forward corner (tack) and reduce its efficiency there. See figure 61.

The tension in the foot of the mainsail can also be adjusted by a Cunningham hole device, with a cringle in the foot, but is more commonly controlled by an outhaul at the aft lower corner (clew).

The line for controlling this tension is frequently made fast at the outer end of the boom and is not easily adjusted when sailing, but on high performance boats, particularly those with hollow metal booms, the tensioning line may be taken through a lead at the aft end of the boom, and then forward within the boom to an internal block and tackle system and out through a hole in the boom to a cleat near the forward end, so that adjustments may be made easily when sailing, as in figure 60.

# 13 Other Mainsail Controls

Apart from other considerations, tensioning the mainsail leech by holding the boom down reduces twist in the sail—an important point in heavy weather, as the wind can be spilt from the sail while most of it continues to drive efficiently, rather than nearly all of it flapping impotently like a flag. Twist in the sail encourages the wind flow to run up the sail to escape from the leech higher up and this in itself causes more heeling forces on the sail.

A kicking strap or boom vang—basically a tackle attached at its upper end to the boom about two feet from the gooseneck and at its lower end near the heel of the mast or sometimes to the hull structure below this—are essential as an aid to mainsail leech tensioning and the reduction of twist, as they continue to hold the boom down when the sail is eased right out on a run or broad reach, when even centre mainsheet systems are not very effective. Usually they consist of a quick-release device on the boom attached to a wire rope which is tensioned by a simple tackle or by a winch. Kicking strap winches are generally of the drum and spindle type and may be fitted with a self locking device, so that adjustments are very quickly and easily made.

Battens in the mainsail are intended to spread the leech, to help distribute the tension loads over its area, to hold the leech flat so that the airstream flows off it cleanly with the minimum drag and to prevent it flapping in normal circumstances. Battens should generally be quite stiff except at their forward ends, where flexibility may be increased to allow them to follow the curve of the sail and prevent them causing a 'hard spot' or ridge down the sail. Battens are usually slipped into pockets and their length should be suitable to the length of the pocket; if forced in under slight compression, the batten will make the sail curve—probably desirable with the top batten. Battens are made from many different materials, but wood is probably the most satisfactory, as they can then be tapered easily to give precisely the right degree of flexibility, which is very important.

# 14 Jib Controls

The forward edge (luff) of jibs is sleeved over a wire rope. This wire rope is intended to be as non-stretch as possible and, though the sail is normally seized to it so that relative movement is eliminated, in some cases the sail is only seized to the wire at the head, the sleeve being

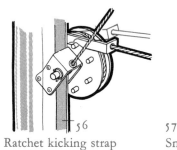

56
Ratchet kicking strap
winch

57
Snap shackle for spinnaker
sheets or halyards

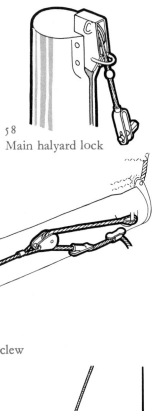

58
Main halyard lock

59
Jib furling drum

60
Internal outhaul for mainsail clew

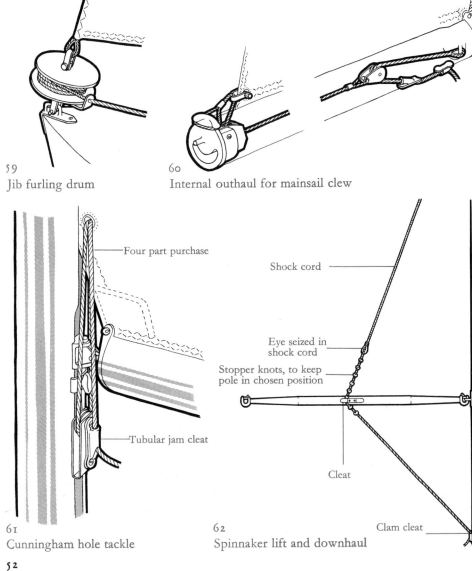

Four part purchase

Tubular jam cleat

61
Cunningham hole tackle

Shock cord

Eye seized in
shock cord

Stopper knots, to keep
pole in chosen position

Cleat

Clam cleat

62
Spinnaker lift and downhaul

free to travel on the wire and permitting independent alterations to the tension in the luff of the sail by using a Cunningham hole arrangement. Though doubtless this recently introduced further control of the shape of the jib will be widely used in some top-performing boats, the necessity of its being remotely adjustable adds to its complications and it is impossible to use it in conjunction with jib furling gears, which roll the jib on its luff rope by revolving it like a roller blind.

Other devices are in more common use to assist in controlling the shape of jibs. For instance, the jib halyard may emerge from the foot of the mast and be taken up to a lever mounted further up; an eye in the halyard is slipped over a hook extending from the lever, so that actuating the lever, which is self-locking, increases the tension on the halyard and hence on the luff of the jib. The lever is generally able to slide in a track and, though not readily adjustable while racing, may be clamped in different positions during the tuning-up process. The jib luff is kept straight only by tension, slackening of the halyard resulting in concave curvature of the luff and increased flow or camber in the sail.

When sailing, the flexing of the mast, stretch in rigging and flexing of the hull make it impossible to maintain the tension originally put in the jib luff, for as soon as the lee shroud becomes slack (which it always does) the forward pull of the jib luff is no longer counter-balanced by the aft pull of the two shrouds and the principal factor then maintaining jib luff tension is tension in the leech of the mainsail, pulling the masthead aft. As this aft pull is transmitted through the topmast, the latter's relative length is important. All this leads to the conclusion that a properly designed rig partly automatically adjusts the jib luff tension by means of the mainsail leech tension, controlled by mainsheet tension. The main function of the jib halyard lever, therefore, is not to increase the tension on the jib luff, but to ease it in light weather, when more luff curvature is required to increase the camber in the sail.

The set of the jib is also affected by the fore and aft position of the jib sheet fairlead. This should normally be positioned so that the line of the sheet, if extended forward, meets the luff of the jib about 12 inches above a line bisecting the angle at the clew (aft corner) of the sail. Moving the fairlead forward tightens the leech, reduces flow in the head of the sail, reduces twist and increases flow in the foot. Moving it aft does the reverse. Fairleads sliding in tracks allow their position to be adjusted easily, but are not vital equipment, as once the right position has been found it is best not to move them.

# 15 Spinnaker Controls

Spinnakers are also very susceptible to the tension put on their edges. A properly shaped spinnaker spreads itself remarkably efficiently, but to do this the edges of the sail must be at the correct tension. The sheet-lead positions for the spinnaker are therefore important. It is also essential to be able to control the height of the outboard end of the spinnaker boom, to which the tack of the sail is attached. This is done by a spinnaker boom lift, to raise it, and a spinnaker boom vang to pull it down. The lift and vang are attached to a cleat or eye at the centre of the spinnaker pole. The lift may be elastic shock cord or, to give better control, a light line led through a fairlead on the mast and down the mast to a cleat. The boom vang takes considerable strain and is normally a Terylene cord taken through a fairlead at about deck level, either on the mast or on the deck just by the mast, thence to a cleat. Often the vang and lift are joined, so that if the lift is shock cord it automatically snaps the whole device back to the mast as soon as it is released from the spinnaker pole. This arrangement is shown in figure 62.

# 16 Rigging

Rigging is divided into two categories: standing rigging—which supports the mast and includes shrouds and forestay; and running rigging which hoists and adjusts the sails or spars and includes such items as halyards and sheets.

## a Standing rigging

This is almost invariably wire rope, though occasionally solid wire is used. The wire rope may be galvanised plough-steel or stainless steel, the latter being far preferable because the protective zinc coating on plough-steel wire is very thin.

The most common forms of construction are 7 × 7 and 1 × 19. The 7 × 7 construction is seven strands made up of seven wires each. 1 × 19 is a single strand of nineteen wires. 1 × 19 is greatly superior to the other construction as it stretches less, is smoother and less wind resistant, and the individual wires are thicker and less susceptible to damage. It can be ruined by kinking and it is slightly more difficult to make a strong joint to it, as clamped or swaged collars and fittings do not grip quite so firmly on its smoother surface.

The commonest ends in standing rigging are eyes formed round stainless steel thimbles, with the wire rope clamped back on itself by means of a ferrule. The ferrule is a thick-walled tube about half-inch long, through which the wires are slid and which is then squeezed up tightly on to the wires in an hydraulic press (Talurit process). For most purposes a copper ferrule is best, brass being too hard and aluminium alloy too soft. The eye so formed is usually attached to its fitting with a stainless steel clevis pin, secured by a split pin.

It is neater and causes less wind resistance if the end fittings are swaged (squeezed) directly on to the wire. This is done by having a hollow socket in the fitting into which the wire is pushed, the socket then being clamped tightly on the wire by a special tool. Swaged end fittings are slightly more expensive than thimbled eyes, but stainless steel end fittings swaged to 1 × 19 stainless wire rope are virtually everlasting. The length of standing rigging may be altered either by rigging screws or by adjustable shroud plates. A rigging screw is nearly always used for the forestay. Rigging screws tend to become unwound during sailing unless clamped tightly with lock nuts or by some other means. Once the boat has been properly tuned, frequent alterations to the rigging screws should be unnecessary and the lock nuts can then be tightened very securely and taped up, only the forestay being slackened when the mast is taken down.

In some very simple boats, including those for junior sailing, there may be no means of adjusting the shrouds. This is sometimes inconvenient, as even the most simple boats can benefit from tuning. The old fashioned rigging lanyard is a very good system for children's boats, particularly now that Terylene, which does not shrink or stretch, can be used. One of the advantages is that if there is difficulty in righting the boat with the mast and sails in position after a capsize, the lanyards may easily be cut and the whole lot removed, though with proper buoyancy equipment this should never be necessary.

## b Running rigging

Halyards for mainsail and jib must not stretch more than is unavoidable. Mainly for this reason, wire rope is used as much as possible, but it is not easy to cleat and cleating soon kinks and ruins it, so normally a fibre-rope tail is spliced onto the wire so that the wire stops just short of the cleat on to which the tail is made fast.

Sometimes the wire rope ends in a soft eye (without a thimble). This is slipped on to a halyard hook, the halyard being tensioned by some other device. With this method the sail is hoisted by a light jockey halyard attached to the wire rope, but this carries no load once the sail is up and the wire halyard is hooked.

Tension on the mainsail luff is usually applied after the halyard has been set up, by using a gooseneck fitting which can be adjusted in height, or by means of a Cunningham hole fitting. Another more sophisticated device is the main halyard lock, in which a steel ball is swaged on to the halyard near the end which is attached to the head of the mainsail; this stainless steel ball engages in a catch fitted to the top of the mast, as in figure 58.

The specially flexible wire rope (7 × 19) used for jib or main halyards is constructed of six strands, each of nineteen very thin wires, formed round a seventh strand as core. Stainless steel is not always satisfactory for halyards, tending to be brittle, so that individual wires break where they are severely stressed and flexed passing over sheaves, forming jagged whiskers sticking out of the wire, which can rip hands. Galvanised wire rope is generally preferable, though its life is rather limited. Halyard sheaves should not be less than one inch in diameter.

Flying Dutchman  Designer: W. van Essen
Photographer: Eileen Ramsay

Five-O-Five  Designer: John Westell
Photographer: Eileen Ramsay

Hornet  Designer: Jack Holt
Photographer: Trevor Davies

Fireball  Designer: Peter Milne
Photographer: Eileen Ramsay

To overcome the short life and difficulties of cleating wire ropes, a prestretched Terylene rope is manufactured and often used in simpler boats, but it stretches more, is bulkier, slightly heavier when dry and a good deal heavier when wet, and is more wind resistant, so is not generally used on high performance boats.

Nearly all the fibre cordage on sailing boats these days is Terylene. Terylene forms immensely strong ropes, is rot-proof, very resistant to abrasion and wear, remains soft and pliable when wet and does not shrink on to cleats. It is made in many different forms to suit all purposes. Vegetable-fibre ropes are used on cheap boats but, apart from lower first cost, are completely outclassed by synthetic-fibre types. Spinnaker halyards should be Terylene made from continuous filament with a smooth shiny surface, which easily runs over sheaves and fairleads. Sheets, on the other hand, are best made from short filament Terylene, soft plaited, giving a slightly fluffy finish which is easier to grip with cold wet hands. Plaited construction is ideal for sheets, as it renders smoothly through blocks, is very flexible, and has no tendency at all to kink. The rope used for sheets should be fairly thick, even though it may be infinitely stronger than necessary, to provide a comfortable and efficient grip. Thin sheets are an abomination as they cut into the hands.

For some functions stranded rope is better than plaited, providing a slightly better grip. It is normally used for halyard tails.

Ropes are also made from Courlene, polythene and nylon which all have special characteristics. Polythene ropes are buoyant and are therefore suitable for mooring ropes and towing warps. Nylon has a high degree of elasticity, making it suitable for the bolt ropes on the edges of sails and for anchor lines.

# 17 Fittings

Fittings on the boat are of two main types:

1  Those essential to the working of the boat.
2  Those for the added comfort and convenience of the crew.

These two categories are closely interrelated, because an inconvenienced and uncomfortable crew cannot really sail efficiently.

The positioning of fittings in the boat is most important. For instance, there is no excuse for positioning jib fairleads just where the crew cannot avoid sitting on them. The sail plan should be designed to make this unnecessary.

The fittings comprise a fairly large proportion of the cost of the boat and inevitably there is a temptation to skimp on quality. In many cases, however, the safety of the boat depends on the fittings as much as anything else and not only should they be properly designed and manufactured, in the correct material, but also they obviously should be correctly and securely fastened.

Reinforced nylon is increasingly used to produce cheap lightweight

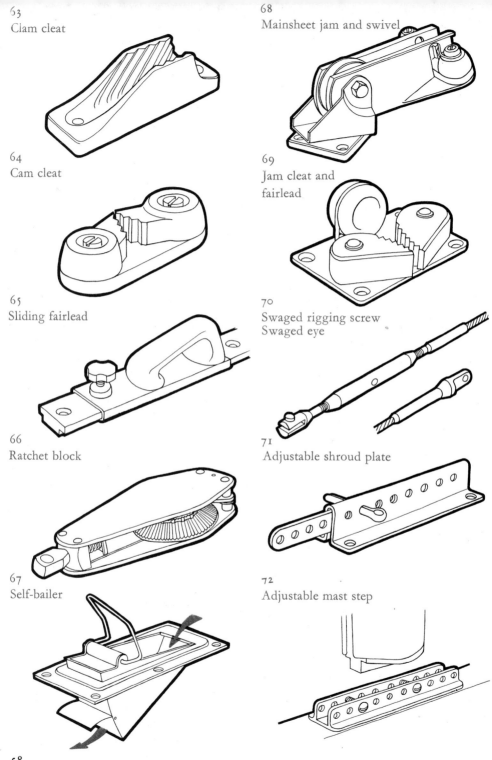

63
Clam cleat

64
Cam cleat

65
Sliding fairlead

66
Ratchet block

67
Self-bailer

68
Mainsheet jam and swivel

69
Jam cleat and fairlead

70
Swaged rigging screw
Swaged eye

71
Adjustable shroud plate

72
Adjustable mast step

fittings, many of which are excellent, though they are sometimes wrongly applied. Stainless steel is usually preferable to light-alloy for fittings which are heavily stressed, particularly when the light-alloy fittings are die-castings. However, anodised light-alloy die-castings are suitable in certain applications, including cam and other cleats. Anodising light-alloy not only protects it from corrosion, but also hardens the surface. Special 'hard anodised' surfaces are extremely tough and even harder than stainless steel but, of course, the process only changes the surface of the material to a very limited depth.

Some crewing aids, such as cam-cleats or snubbing winches for the jib sheets, are quite suitable on cruising dinghies, but less suitable for racing boats in which the sails undergo almost constant trimming. If such cleats are fitted, they should be positioned so that their use is not obligatory. This usually means having the cleats positioned some distance from the fairlead; cleats combined with fairleads should usually be avoided.

Great assistance in handling both jib sheets and main-sheets is given by spring-loaded ratchet blocks. These permit the sheet to be pulled in freely, but bring the ratchet into operation at a preset load, so that the sheet will not run out again freely when this load is reached. Reducing tension on the sheet disengages the ratchet and allows the sheet to run out freely. The sheet itself runs over a serrated sheave to grip the rope and this causes more than usual wear on the rope, but the advantages out-weigh this small disadvantage. See figure 66.

Several types of self-bailer are now available, the most efficient being in the form of a flap which can be pushed down from the bottom of the boat. However, this position makes them liable to be trodden on and damaged, and if possible they should be fitted beneath the thwart or in some relatively protected position, though of course the main consideration is to have them placed so that they drain the boat effectively. This type is shown in figure 67.

# 18 Live Ballast

Because the main stabilising factor in a light sailing boat is the disposition of the crew, it is most important to use the crew's weight to the best advantage—and least disadvantage—to balance the heeling forces on the sails.

In light airs, helmsman and crew must be able to move their weight easily and smoothly, without violently rocking the boat and shaking what little wind there is out of the sails. For this reason the centre thwart should be at a convenient height to enable the crew to slide his weight across it. Side benches should be high enough to let the crew sit in reasonable comfort and to enable him to get up quickly with little effort, to sit on the gunwale or move to the other side of the boat, rather than having to hoist himself up as though getting out of a low armchair. On the other hand, side benches must not cut into the back

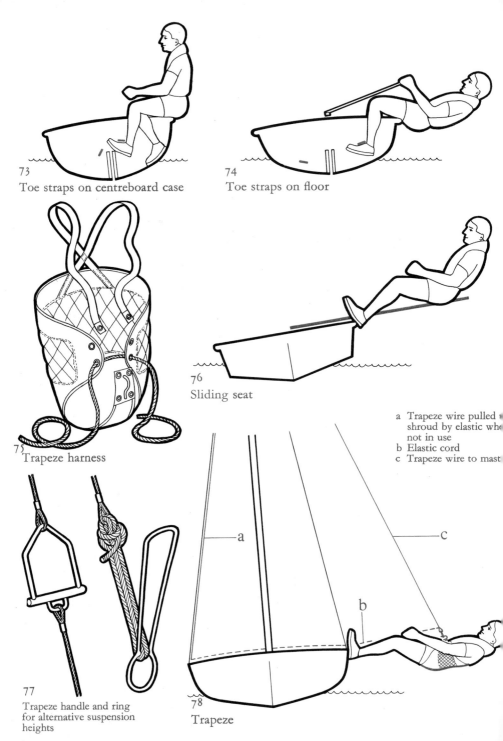

73
Toe straps on centreboard case

74
Toe straps on floor

75
Trapeze harness

76
Sliding seat

a  Trapeze wire pulled
   shroud by elastic whe
   not in use
b  Elastic cord
c  Trapeze wire to mast

a

c

b

77
Trapeze handle and ring
for alternative suspension
heights

78
Trapeze

of the legs when the crew is sitting on the gunwale. The gunwale itself should be wide enough to be reasonably comfortable. Decks should be narrow enough not to cut into the back of legs and the edges rounded. It is essential also that the crew does not slip and fall about in the boat. Smooth, wet surfaces, particularly of GRP, are slippery even to modern grip-sole sailing shoes. Non-skid material, such as Trakmark, should be applied in strips wherever necessary. There may be shrinkage, stretch and adhesion problems if these materials are applied in large pieces. In GRP boats non-skid patterns may be incorporated in the moulding, but care has to be taken to ensure that they will release easily from the mould and that they do not cause voids immediately under the surface. Minnesota Mining Materials make an extremely efficient sandpaper-like material that is ideal for floors, but it should not be used where it will chafe bare skin or clothes.

The most obvious use to which the crew's weight can be put is to get it as far outboard as possible on the windward side, to balance the heeling forces on the sails. But there is more to it than that. It is no good leaving him perched far out over the side but unable to get back into the boat quickly if the wind suddenly eases — the boat will merely capsize on top of him.

The three main aids to using the crew as live ballast as far outboard as possible are:

1   Toe straps

The most simple arrangement, merely enabling the crew to sit with the gunwale or deck edge under his thighs and lean back, so that his body is parallel with the water, as shown in figure 74. Toe straps are usually fastened to the centreboard case and the underside of the thwart, but in some cases, in order to get the weight still further out (and with wider boats), the toe straps may be fastened to the floor of the boat. Toe straps should always be very firmly secured by plates and should be of rot-proof non-stretch webbing (eg Terylene). Machine belting is sometimes used for floor fastened toe straps, because this is stiff enough to stand up in loops under which the feet can easily be slipped. It is inclined to be harsh on wet skin, but can be padded with foamed plastic.

2   Sliding seats

Used in the National Hornet and in several single-handers, including Minisail, International Canoe and Toy Classes. Canoe slides are extremely long and real experts use them to the maximum—sitting right on the outboard end and tucking their knees under their chin to get the weight of their legs even further out. This needs great skill. Hornet sliding seats are much shorter, but sufficiently long for a crew sitting on the end of the seat with his legs at full stretch, to have his feet just on the gunwale. Minisail sliding seats (not always used) are shorter still, but their effect is quite great in so small a boat. Sliding seats considerably reduce the physical strain on the crew when sitting

Jiffy  Designer: Ian Proctor
Photographer: Archie Handford Ltd

Optimist  Designer: Clark Mills
Photographer: Eileen Ramsay

Cadet  Designer: Jack Holt
Photographer: Eileen Ramsay

Gull  Designer: Ian Proctor
Photographer: Eileen Ramsay

out, but do, of course, demand more activity in tacking, when the crew has to come in from the seat, slide it across to the other side and then get out on it.

### 3 Trapezes

Consist of a canvas belt or sling round the body of the crew, with a hook or latch at the front, engaging with a specially shaped ring attached to a wire suspended from high up the mast on each side. The crew hooks himself on to the wire, squats with his feet on the edge of the deck and then pushes outwards, so that he is suspended over the side by the wire, with his feet on the edge of the gunwale. Usually there is an elastic cord attached to the ring on the wire, so that when not in use the wire is held taut in line with the shrouds and does not swing about; the crew can then easily grab the ring to hook himself on and simply pushes outwards, the shock cord stretching to permit this.

There is a little more physical strain with trapezes than with sliding seats, as the wire is trying to pull the crew in towards the mast and quite a lot of load is put on the forward leg. It is, however, far easier to make adjustments in the position of the crew simply by flexing the knees. It is also possible for a trapezing crew to move his weight aft to help the boat lift up into a plane, and this is the chief advantage over sliding seats, in which fore and aft movement is limited.

It is sometimes claimed that sliding seats and trapezes are particularly helpful to lightweight crews, as in heavy weather they are then better able to keep the boat upright. This claim tends to be fallacious, for the help lightweights may get is even more advantageous to heavyweights in strong winds, because the greater leverage which is given to their weight makes it still more effective.

# 19 Junior Sailing

Though boats for young people need to be safe, they must also be interesting. A child soon becomes bored with a little tub that is a sluggard in anything other than fresh winds. Though some children are content just to sail or race, the majority want far more from their boats than this, and to broaden their skills and training, the boat should be able to be rowed and sculled as well as just sailed. It can then be a pirate ship or a Roman galley, or storm the Normandy beachhead. The purely racing boat often produces a type of dinghy sailor who knows little of the varied art of seamanship. He may be able to go out and win races, but possibly brings his boat into the shore like a steam train running amok.

It is a mistake for the boat to be too large for the child concerned. It will be difficult to handle in and out of the water and, for it to have a reasonable performance for its size, the sail area will be too large for the child to manage without strain.

The boat should be easily rigged and, except in the case of very small sails such as in the Optimist and Jiffy, the easiest rig is Bermuda.

Quite a number of children's boats are gunter or lug rigged, but in both cases rigging may become difficult as soon as the yard is hoisted sufficiently far for the wind to start blowing the sail about.

Very young children are better off with only one sail to manage. Usually this is positioned well forward on the boat, and if so the hull should be amply buoyant in the bows so that if the child has to go forward to attend to the sail, the stability of the boat is not seriously affected. Obviously there should also be ample buoyancy apparatus, properly disposed fore and aft. There should be a dropping rudder to facilitate sailing on and off shore. Mast (and yard) should both be buoyant to help prevent the boat turning turtle in a capsize.

As the trickiest point of sailing a small boat is running in a strong wind, when a very short hull may be directionally unstable, a skeg aft to steady the boat on its course is helpful. A skeg also provides a good hand-hold on a capsized boat.

Rowing positions should be suitable for short arms and short legs. Rowlocks should be about 8 inches forward of the thwart or seat on which the rower sits and convenient foot rests should be provided if possible. The seating should be high enough to give the child a proper chance to pull the oars using his weight and back muscles as well as his arms rather than having his hands high above his shoulders as he makes the stroke.

Rowlocks should be able to be attached to the boat so that they do not get lost or fall out during a capsize. It must be possible to lower the sails easily. The sculling notch in the transom should be deep, and it is helpful if it is not a mere semicircle but has an inch or so of vertical side against which the oar can bear without jumping out of the notch. There should be something to which a painter may be made fast.

Older children soon want the added interest of a jib and may get bored unless there is a sail for each of them to handle. A jib of about 20 square feet is usually quite big enough for a crew of around 12 years old to manage.

# 20 Girl and Junior Crews

Some boats demand too much physical strength from the jibsheet hand to make them suitable for crewing by normal women or young people. The maximum size of jib which can be handled efficiently by most women is about 30 square feet and very often they appreciate not having to deal with a spinnaker.

Generally speaking, the smaller lightweight boats with a small sail area and without spinnakers are more suitable for sailing with girl crews, as the boats can be more easily handled ashore and do not require such vigorous sitting-out over such a wide range of wind speeds. This is the reason for the popularity as husband and wife boats of the National Twelves, Fireflies and Graduates. Lightweight crews are at an advantage in National Twelves in particular.